HOW TO SURVIVE THE CORONAVIRUS RECESSION

HS Press

RYUHO OKAWA

HOW TO
SURVIVE
THE
CORONAVIRUS
RECESSION

HS PRESS

Copyright © 2020 by Ryuho Okawa
English translation © Happy Science 2020
Original title: *Corona Fukyoka no Survival Jutsu*

HS Press is an imprint of IRH Press Co., Ltd.
Tokyo
ISBN 13: 978-1-943869-97-8
ISBN 10: 1-943869-97-9
Cover Image: Khun Zaw Min Tun/shutterstock.com
aquariagirl1970/shutterstock.com

Contents

Preface 13

CHAPTER ONE

How to Survive the Coronavirus Recession

1 **My Thoughts during This Time of Coronavirus Crisis**

"How to survive" for good people 16

Be careful of what you see on newspapers and TV 17

Work to build a society where people are allowed to give different opinions 19

Even large businesses must think of ways to survive 20

Hospitals and doctors' offices are "failing" because there are too many "customers" 22

The current trend works against the principle of economy 24

Don't rely too much on compensation 25

2 Overcoming Fear of the Novel Coronavirus

There are fewer cases of infections and deaths from it compared to those from influenza 27

Almost all industries are closing, so even fox spirits are "unemployed" 28

The coronavirus trouble is partially instigated by fear 30

People should be able to work freely so that they don't take their own lives 31

Try to work to fulfill your mission from God 33

Focus your mind on making others happy, not on fear or self-preservation 34

Realize that the soul is eternal and regain your true self as a human being 36

It's also important to accept your lifespan given by God 37

3 Survive by Strengthening Your Immunity and Taking Other Measures

The government lacks a wider perspective and is at a loss against the coronavirus 39

Strengthen your immunity by developing your willpower, living cheerfully, and training your body 41

Disinfecting your body by drinking green tea or rooibos tea, and keeping good hygiene by washing your hands 44

The Japanese custom regarding a meal can help prevent you from getting infected 46

Japan's sanitary culture should spread more around the world 47

There isn't much need for masks in non-crowded places 49

4 Don't Be Afraid to Work

"Closed country" policies will invite serious repercussions 51

The government won't save you 53

Stay strong, both mentally and physically 55

Regulations should be eased 56

What you should do while you stay at home 58

5 Aim to Survive through Religious Power

Happy Science music and movies keep you away from
spiritual disturbances and viral infections 60

Imagine that you are purifying the path you walk 61

You should have the right faith and spread the Truth 62

Happy Science publications on the coronavirus match
public demand 64

Happy Science Kigan is an "unknown attack" against
viruses 66

I hope good-hearted people will survive by dint of religious
power 68

CHAPTER TWO

How to Strengthen Your Immunity

1 **This Is a Vaccine by My Spiritual Power**

    People with a weak immune system easily die from the
novel coronavirus 72

    Creating a religious vaccine from my spiritual power 74

2 **Abandon Your Fear and Be Positive**

    A viral infection is the same as spiritual possession 76

    Your fear attracts what you fear 77

    People with an aura are difficult to be possessed 79

    Think cheerfully, positively, affirmatively, and
constructively 80

3 **The Spiritual Truth behind the Virus Infection**

    How to recover from a viral infection is the same as
expelling evil spirits 82

    A lost spirit is at the heart of a viral infection outbreak 83

    With spiritual power, you can transfer the evil spirit with
the virus to others 85

4 Maintaining a Good Mental and Physical Condition

Vaccination may not be effective even if developed 86

Quit eating unhealthily, and have a healthy, balanced diet 88

5 Spiritual Causes of Allergies and Ways to Overcome Them

An example of recovery from an allergy through self-reflection 90

Allergic reactions can arise from fearful experiences from your past lives 91

If you live with superstitions, your body may react to them 92

Your knowledge and past-experience can be the reason for your allergic reactions 93

Animals have spirit bodies 94

Don't be too attached to your pets that have died 97

The effects of joining the events of Happy Science 100

6 The Secret to Strengthen Your Immunity and Fight against Viruses

Your belief in God becomes your immunity 103

Meditation also has the power to fight viruses 105

Balanced nutrition and occasional exercise are also important 106

A malicious pandemic spreads when there are many political issues 107

Let's stay healthy and help the world prosper 109

CHAPTER THREE

Current View on the Coronavirus Infection
Q&A Session on the Lecture, "My Philosophy of Life"

1 **Coronavirus Is No Different Than the Flu** 112
  Comparing various opinions until a conclusion is found ... 113
  Politicians do exactly as they are told by some epidemiologists 114
  An epidemiologist who maintains that infectious disease does not actually exist 115
  Is there a need to be this cautious of the coronavirus? 116
  The novel coronavirus should be weak against sunlight and fresh air 118

2 **Protect Yourself**
  Do not depend on the government 120
  Healthy people should work 123
  Think from various angles 125
  Make your own judgments of your own problems 126

3 **The Qualities Expected of a Leader**
  The government should not do things that discourage people from helping each other 129
  The government should come up with places that people can go 132
  Work to gain wider and higher recognition as you are promoted 133
  Leaders must take responsibility for their words and decisions 134

Afterword 137

Miracle Healing 140

About the Author 143
What Is El Cantare? 144
What Is a Spiritual Message? 146
About Happy Science 150
About Happy Science Movies 154
Contact Information 156
About Happiness Realization Party 158
About IRH Press USA 159
Books by Ryuho Okawa 160
Music by Ryuho Okawa 170

Preface

Indeed, we have entered an age of survival. In Japan, there have been only over 10,000 infected cases and several hundred deaths, but the administration is spending quite a lot of energy as if they want to avoid taking responsibility for their miserable failure to secure the economic boom that the Tokyo Olympics was expected to bring.

A state of emergency was declared for about a month, and it left microbusinesses, small and medium-sized businesses, and large businesses seemingly possessed by Grim Reapers, gods of destruction, gods of bankruptcy, and gods of poverty.

If an administration follows the opinions of epidemiologists, then the principles of economics, fundamental human rights, and democratic politics will be destroyed. In Japan, a country with strong peer pressure, many people will die due to hunger and suicide, and the nation's finances will fail. Even if the administration offers a "scapegoat" to reduce people's dissatisfaction or let them vent, that won't solve the problem.

The way to survive the coronavirus recession is similar to a fight against totalitarianism: If each of you doesn't make progress in your work through your wisdom and effort, act two of this tragedy will result. Please read this book carefully.

Ryuho Okawa
Master & CEO of Happy Science Group
May 21, 2020

CHAPTER ONE

How to Survive the Coronavirus Recession

*Originally recorded in Japanese on April 22, 2020,
in the Special Lecture Hall of Happy Science in Japan,
and later translated into English.*

1

My Thoughts during This Time of Coronavirus Crisis

"How to survive" for good people

This chapter is titled, "How to Survive the Coronavirus Recession." Regarding this, I have too much to say all at once. The situation is always changing, so I must add more as things happen and give my opinion on them.

I could talk about executive management in general, but since the central and local governments are using laws and ordinances to do what they want one-sidedly, it's difficult for me to talk about executive management in the usual sense. Now they are working in unison with the mass media, so if what they are doing is wrong, this whole country will most likely fail.

Let me give a brief overview of the situation. The central government declared a state of emergency, which applied to the whole nation later. Two weeks have passed, but the situation is not very good. It seems that much more bad than good is to be expected, so recently, I have felt that the Abe administration, which has been in power for long, will fail terribly in its final days.

I will try to talk using simple words, but it's difficult to talk about a way to survive that applies to everyone. So, in this chapter, I'll shift my focus to "having good people survive," with the hope that they survive. With the way things are going now, I sometimes think, "Maybe all bad people should be wiped out. Maybe bad people, bad occupations, and bad businesses shouldn't survive. That might be OK."

I just want right-minded people, people who live by the Truth, and people who are trying to live for the world to survive. So, I want not only Happy Science members but also non-members who are good-hearted or good-natured to read this book. As for those who have absolutely no interest in listening to what I want to say, I won't bother.

Be careful of what you see on newspapers and TV

Especially now, you can see many reports on the number of additional infected cases and deaths due to the novel coronavirus in newspapers and on the news and talk shows every day. They even give the numbers for different local regions. But if you watch them every day, you will tend to think that nothing will get better and that you will only see more infected cases. This is not good for your mental health. It would seem as if only darkness lay ahead.

Of course, there is some information you need, so it's OK to watch just a part of the news or briefly read the summaries of the news, but you shouldn't watch or read too much of them in detail. Something is just increasing little by little, every day. That's all. But through this, the public is being psychologically manipulated, which I think is dangerous.

Please excuse me for sounding sarcastic, but nowadays, I see doctors who don't usually appear in newspapers and on TV and other media, especially those who work closely with infections, showing up frequently and giving a lot of their opinions. But they are experts in their own limited fields. They might have opinions to give regarding things that involve their work, but they almost don't think about the effects their opinions could have on the overall structure or action, such as the nation's management, economy, politics, trade, and interactions with other nations. Therefore, just because they are experts in a field doesn't mean their opinions should be applied to everything. There is a mistake in such a way of thinking.

Work to build a society where people are allowed to give different opinions

In the U.S., President Trump is thinking that they should soon start working to revive their economy, but the mass media is mocking him, saying that he's the most unscientific or anti-science president they've ever had. Hearing that, I felt that Happy Science was in a very similar state to that of President Trump. Oftentimes, what he calls "fake news" is also "fake news" to us. We are alike.

When someone says something that goes against what everyone else thinks and does as common sense, people tend to want to organize a "witch hunt" or bully the person, but I think this is a trend to watch out for. We must be a society where people are allowed to give opinions or take actions that are different from what people usually say or do. It's dangerous to only accept one way of thinking. We must not "hunt witches" or bury such people when they appear.

Even doctors, who are experts, have very little experience regarding this kind of worldwide pandemic. It's something that may or may not happen once in your lifetime. People who lived through the Great Depression in 1929 and are still living today would be over 91 years old, and they were babies at the time, so they wouldn't remember anything about it. Those who remember such days would be over 100 years old, and I believe there are very few of those. Therefore, we can say there will be no experience to rely on. Everything we do is like searching in the dark based on our imagination.

Especially now, people prefer a macro-level perspective using large numbers. Many of them without making value judgments say, "This is how it will be," so we must be careful. We must imagine how each case will be, case by case.

Even large businesses must think of ways to survive

Two weeks have passed since Japan declared a state of emergency, but the government is saying, "We still need to wait one or two weeks to see its effects." Two weeks ago, the government said that the state of emergency would be in effect until May 6, but everyone felt in their subconscious that it would be extended. Even children didn't believe the pandemic would be settled.

If it could be settled in just one month, the government might be able to give financial aid for closure or unemployment or provide compensation to companies, but this will be nearly impossible if the situation lasts for more than three months. Companies will go bankrupt, and not just small businesses, but also large ones. Large businesses, medium-sized businesses, micro-businesses, and sole proprietorships will all fail, so you must think of a way to survive. People who can give their own opinions are needed. Otherwise, the public will likely give the government full authority, which is something to be careful of.

Perhaps Prime Minister Abe is feeling as if invisible "virus bombs" are attacking Japan every night. He might be thinking like this: "We are being attacked from above. Bombs are being dropped on us, so please take shelter in your homes. Take cover by going into the basement of the sturdiest building you can find." To me, it sounds as if he is telling us, "Spread out as much as possible and hide, because if you crowd together, many of you will die all at once"; "Don't use the public transit system because many of you will die if it is targeted"; or "If you evacuate to the countryside, the population density there will go up, and it could be bombed. So, don't evacuate there, but instead, hide underground in the large cities."

I might have sounded slightly sarcastic, so some of you may be shocked, but I needed to say those things because they are hard to understand unless they are said in an extreme way.

Hospitals and doctors' offices are "failing" because there are too many "customers"

Recently, doctors have been appearing on TV as commentators, which is something to be worried about. To tell the truth, hospitals and doctors' offices are thriving. They are actually thriving to the point that they are "failing" because there are too many "customers." That is the reality.

What happens when they accept more patients than they are supposed to? The answer is that doctors won't be able to check patients' health conditions because they have accepted more patients than they are supposed to. This occurs because they are understaffed, which means the staff is overworking without any days off, and because they are short of equipment, food, and so on. It's similar to the case that happened years ago—there was food poisoning at a traditional Japanese inn because it accepted too many customers. More recently, we saw people quarantined on the cruise ship docked in Tokyo Bay. I believe hospitals are experiencing something like that. Please forgive me if I sounded rude for saying that hospitals and doctors' offices are accepting too many "customers," but I wanted to make it easier for you to understand.

Some hospitals have even lined up beds in corridors to accept patients, and others have put up tents outside to conduct tests there since they cannot let any more patients inside the building. Medical workers are afraid that the patients coming in to get tested will infect them and other patients, so now, people are gradually coming to dislike people.

The same thing is happening to people who travel. Some think that people who travel with others are due to get infected, as are those who go to the countryside. It might be OK to think that way for the time being, but when the time comes to try to bring back the economy, people will not visit such places. They will think, "You told us not to come. You rejected us." Then, there will gradually be fewer people who go to those places, so it will be difficult to recover.

The current trend works against the principle of economy

"Infection spreads when crowds gather." We hear this often nowadays, but it goes against the principle of economy. To put it straight and simple, the principle of economy is "sales = price per unit × number of units sold." The amount from sales is the price of the product per unit of the item or service times the number of people or units bought. Now, the number of people or units is being reduced by about 80 percent, which is quite a heavy restriction. If the price became five times higher than what it was, then you could expect the same amount from sales, but such a thing won't happen.

For example, take the foodservice industry, which is suffering heavily. If the number of customers drops to 20 percent of what it used to be, restaurants and other shops can't raise their prices to five times what they are set at now. If they did, people would choose not to go there. They would rather buy ingredients at a supermarket and cook them at home, so they wouldn't eat out. Therefore, restaurants and shops can't raise their prices. In this way, the principle of the economy can't be applied as it usually would be.

Don't rely too much on compensation

When I was watching the news yesterday (April 21), I saw foodservice workers complaining that they would go bankrupt if the situation continued as it was. They were saying something like, "The foodservice industry has three costs: material, labor, and rent. If we don't provide food, we can eliminate material costs, but we must pay for labor and rent. So, we hope the government will change the legal system and provide us with compensation for rent." But I don't think this is possible.

Perhaps it is possible if there is an end date. For example, it would be doable if they were asking to be given compensation for rent until May 6, but there is no way the government can keep providing compensation when no one knows the date the regulations will be lifted. This is true for all countries. Some might say, "We hope the owners will give all tenants free rent," but this would mean that the owners of the real estate would go bankrupt. Therefore, you can expect quite a difficult situation to continue.

2

Overcoming Fear of the Novel Coronavirus

There are fewer cases of infections and deaths from it compared to those from influenza

Now, let's ask ourselves, "How many people will die of the coronavirus infection?" Please check that. In Japan, over 10,000 people have been infected as of today (April 22), but the number of deaths is much smaller. The mortality rate is just a few percent. On the other hand, if we look at the numbers due to influenza, they are much higher. When the flu goes around, we see one or two million people get infected, which calls for classrooms to shut down, and from several thousand up to 10,000 people die.

Compared to that, fewer people are dying of the coronavirus and a much smaller number of people being infected. People are being told not to go outside, which could be one reason, but it's, indeed, a small number. As for the mortality rate around the world, it's somewhere from 5 to just under 10 percent. Also, the elderly as well as the disabled are apt to die from pneumonia or other complications. This effect is not much different from that of influenza.

By the way, let me ask you a question: What do you usually do when the flu goes around? How do you spend your money, work at your job, and live your life? You might wear a mask, but I don't think there will be much difference other than that.

Some classrooms might indeed be shut down, but that happens if the infection is widespread in the school. They might shut down in such circumstances, but what we are seeing now is something different; classes are shutting down even before the infection spreads.

Almost all industries are closing, so even fox spirits are "unemployed"

So, most educational facilities are closed. Private tutoring schools and preparatory schools are also in trouble. They are open at night, but since people are being told not to go outside even at night, such places might have to close. However, it's not so easy to rebuild them later once they go bankrupt.

Let me tell you about a spiritual phenomenon that I have been experiencing a lot recently, within the last month or so. Fox spirits, or more specifically *youma* (a kind of specter), have been appearing quite often in Taigokan (Master's sacred temple of Happy Science), which is unusual. Why are they coming now, when they usually don't show up here? It seems that the entertainment and amusement districts, such as Ginza, Shimbashi, Shinjuku, Ikebukuro, and Shibuya, which provide nightlife, are all on the verge of closing, so these "helpers" or fox spirits are all being "laid off," too. Each district seems to have laid off more than a thousand fox spirits, and they are hopping around there. The headquarters of Happy Science is located near Gotanda, so there must be quite many of them there, also.

In any case, fox spirits are "unemployed." They do not get a salary, but usually, they enjoy entertaining the customers (by possessing the hosts). They are also delighted when people come to them to pray for business prosperity. But because they've lost their jobs, they've come hopping over to Happy Science. Fox spirits are attacking us as if we were the "boss of raccoon dogs."[1] They seem to be asking for unemployment compensation from us, telling us to do something about the situation since they can't go on like this.

In the old days, fox spirits were able to be reborn into fox bodies, but nowadays, there aren't many wilderness areas, let alone foxes, in Tokyo, so they can't enter such bodies. If there are more *youma*-type humans, foxes can be reborn as humans under some circumstances. There are, however, some cases where animals can be reborn as humans. Anyhow, fox spirits are now upset because they think they are being driven out as a result of the coronavirus issue.

The coronavirus trouble is partially instigated by fear

Religious groups are experiencing tough times because people believe that gathering in groups will spread the virus. In South Korea, a cluster infection occurred twice or more in the churches of a new Christian movement, and this has led people to be very cautious of religious gatherings. Islamic groups are gathering and praying in large spaces, but they are also facing tough times because people think this will easily spread the virus.

Speaking of Christianity, many people get married in churches. A typical wedding can involve about 100 people, which could cause a cluster infection, so people are postponing weddings. The same goes for funerals. Dozens of people gather at a funeral, so it's getting quite difficult to hold one. In this way, religions and religious services are suffering tremendous damage overall.

"People must not gather." This started with large concerts, baseball games, soccer matches, rugby matches, and sumo tournaments being held behind closed doors or even canceled. But as I said earlier, the numbers of infected people and deaths due to the coronavirus aren't particularly higher than those of influenza, so I believe people are being somewhat instigated by fear.

People should be able to work freely so that they don't take their own lives

Now, it seems that the Japanese economy is heading in a direction opposite to that in which Prime Minister Abe has tried to lead it. In a way, this might be the "curse of the consumption tax." He wants people to consume, but they cannot. The government says it will distribute

¥100,000 [about US$ 1,000] to each person who submits an application to receive it, but it is just a drop in the ocean. It might provide some compensation for loss, but most people won't spend that money; they will just save it, so it's meaningless.

Internet shopping sites, especially, are seeing their sales grow slightly, but their competitors, privately-owned retail stores, will most likely be devastated. They are highly likely to close, either temporarily or for good. Some might think, "Let's close down and restart later," but it's difficult to restart a business. If you have your own shop, you might be able to keep it, but if you are paying rent, you will need to cancel the contract and lay off your workers.

Japan is a little behind regarding this, but in the U.S., they are already laying off plenty of people. It was only recently that their unemployment hit the lowest in history, but now, the number is increasing rapidly. It's natural for President Trump to say, "We can't keep going on like this." The protesters, led by Democrats, are taking to the streets and demanding freedom, and a Republican president is supporting that. He encourages them and recommends people be given freedom.

Americans use guns to protect their own homes. They don't expect the police to protect them. These people believe that it's a man's job to shoot down a burglar and protect his family. So, they are saying, "Whether we live or die is up to us to decide. Let us do as we like." I agree.

The reason I agree is that if you remain under restrictions and just stay inactive, your company or business will fail. You could request unemployment compensation, but if you don't receive it, there's nothing you can do about it. This might not lead to more deaths from infections, but it could lead to more suicides instead. In Japan, about 20,000 people take their own lives every year, but considering the current circumstances, this number might grow from this year onward.

Try to work to fulfill your mission from God

There used to be more than 10,000 deaths due to traffic accidents (in Japan). Now, the number has dropped, but even so, several thousand people lose their lives due to such accidents. And, of course, countless people die of many types of illness.

Humans can't choose how they die. Rather, it would be better for them to work to fulfill their mission given by God, by following the basic principle of Buddhism: "Humans are born, they age, get ill, and die. They can't escape the Four Pains of birth, aging, illness, and death."

Leaving hospitals aside, especially now, more people are becoming infected and dying in facilities such as nursing homes. In a way, this could be seen as a solution to the pension problem. So, when we notice this kind of situation, we must check the way our society is working and the way we are treating our families.

Some of you might be targeted by Grim Reapers now. If you think that they have come to "trawl" you and take you away to the other world, then you should think that your time has come, and try to do as many good deeds as possible before you depart for the other world.

Focus your mind on making others happy, not on fear or self-preservation

People die; it's 100 percent true. Science, academic studies, and the opinions of the mass media nowadays don't acknowledge the existence of the other world, but it exists 100 percent.

I have been providing proof of this for over 30 years. Some people mock and ridicule me about that, saying it's absurd, but here's what I want to say to them: "OK, then, please go ahead and let the coronavirus take your life. Then, you can check to see if the other world exists. If it doesn't exist, it's good for you, since you won't have to think about anything anymore. You probably wrote a lot of bad things about me (in weekly tabloids and the like), made plenty of money from them, and enjoyed drinking out at night, but now, you can no longer go out drinking, and you are likely suffering in agony. If so, you should leave this world and experience the other world yourself. But please know that there will be no one to listen to what you have to say."

In history, there have been times when fewer people knew the truth, and those who thought what was true to be false and who spread fake news had more power than those who knew the truth. This is the kind of time we are currently in. So, although it might seem as though you are suffering misfortune, this is also a time when we must rebuild our society.

There will be much misfortune, such as countless

people dying, but here's something to help you perceive the situation in a good way: "People get sick and die. It's something that happens in our everyday life. So, the important thing is to focus your mind on living your limited life meaningfully while trying to make others happy, and not to focus on fear or self-preservation."

Realize that the soul is eternal and regain your true self as a human being

There is a saying, "out of evil comes good." Even if numerous people around the world get infected and die, if people realize that the soul is eternal after seeing how limited life is and if more people start praying or trying to come face to face with God or Buddha, then it will be meaningful. If people learn the limits of the widely acknowledged ideas, "science almighty" and "medicine almighty," and know that they must regain their true selves, then this coronavirus issue will not be in vain.

Now is a time when there are countless humans who utterly ridicule, dismiss, and belittle God or Buddha, arrogantly thinking that they can do everything as they like. These are times when it's completely natural for a disaster to occur. In the books published by Happy Science, it's written that this kind of incident has occurred many times in history.

You won't enjoy the age of arrogance for long, so you need to be humble. This is a good way to perceive the current situation.

It's also important to accept your lifespan given by God

No one wants to die, but everyone must eventually die. You can't choose when you will die, and it can be unfair. Sometimes, good people die early while bad people live longer. However, please know this: you can defend your body to some extent, but beyond that, it will be useless.

Nowadays, about half of Japanese people die from cancer, heart disease, or vascular illness. In earlier days, those who died from cancer must have appeared as if it was due to old age, by heaven's will. Not only cancer but heart disease too, their deaths must have seemed like a natural death due to old age. But now, since doctors extend people's lifespan by giving them treatment, it seems as though they die from an illness. So, sometimes it is important to accept your lifespan given by God.

Animals all have a limited number of years to live. Rabbits, dogs, cats—they all have their own expected lifespan; that's how it is. Turtles might live long, but rabbits don't. It is said that the life expectancy of an animal is related to its maximum number of heartbeats. There is a set number of times an animal's heart can contract in its life, so the animals with a slower rate of contraction will live a long time while those with quicker contractions won't. But the latter can move quicker, so, in other words, their lives are quite fruitful. You could also say that those with less fruitful lives can live longer, but can't accomplish much.

So, now is a time when you should rethink life and death. However, I'm not hoping for there to be some unexpected events where many people die in regret and become lost spirits, so I will make efforts to avoid that.

3

Survive by Strengthening Your Immunity and Taking Other Measures

The government lacks a wider perspective and is at a loss against the coronavirus

You would find it ridiculous if the government were to tell people, in ordinary everyday life, that they must stay at home for about a month, stop going to work or reduce the number of people who go to work by 70 or 80 percent. Like so, what the government is telling us to do now should essentially sound ridiculous to you. They say that cutting the number of people who go to work by 80 percent is an accomplishment, but what are they trying to achieve by doing that? Are they planning on compensating 80 percent of company revenue? Unfortunately, there is no such government, not a single one, that is capable of doing that.

The Japanese government is a bit odd. They raised taxes (in October 2019) and are scattering that money, but to me, they seem as though they want to bring on great destruction like an avalanche. They used to be so worried about people working themselves to death so that when a single person died, they told people to change the way they worked, to go home early on Fridays, and to spend Saturdays and Sundays enjoying recreation. But now, the government is telling us not to go anywhere and to stay at home. This will lead to an outbreak of new diseases, and many people will die. The government is lost as to what to do. They are utterly lacking a wider perspective.

Here is my idea. Basically, we have no choice but to obey laws and regulations. However, let me give you an example. I once saw some video footage of people in India being banned from going outside. I do not know how it is there now since there have been no Japanese media reports on it, but in the footage, a police officer was striking people's legs with a club when they came out of their homes. They were being told not to come out and were struck as physical punishment as if they were horses or cattle.

Perhaps Japan will not go that far, but that is how things will turn out when the law is set. In some places, fines apply, such as in the U.K. There, you will be fined if you hold gatherings of more than two people in public. While this might work in the short term, it's absolutely impossible to do over the long term because it will lead to the destruction of human society.

So, sometimes you must let nature take its course. Things are bound to end at some point. In Sweden, doctors are giving instructions. They are saying something like, "People should be infected in masses. If masses of people are infected at once, many will develop immunity, so they won't pass on the virus. If few people are infected at a time, the infection will last a long time, which is not good. Only the people who survive the mass infection will develop immunity, and that is fine."

As you can see, sometimes different doctors give different instructions, which means people think differently. Some people think, "We will go to work and get infected as a mass. Some of us will die in the blink of an eye, but others will develop immunity and be able to work as usual."

Strengthen your immunity by developing your willpower, living cheerfully, and training your body

The laws set by the government will not cover specific, individual cases, so, as much as you can, please choose how you yourself will survive depending on your occupation and lifestyle. You can be obedient and follow what your country or state says, but in that case, please train your body frequently, so that your life won't end. As much as possible, try to read something that will make you feel brighter, instead of reading, hearing, or watching something that will make you depressed, or close to it. Choose to read novels or watch TV shows that make you feel positive, not negative.

We propose many things, although some mass media sometimes ridicule us, and one or two months after we do, doctors come out with something similar. Simply put, we have been saying, "For the time being, there is no clear measure, vaccine, or shots to defend yourself against the coronavirus pandemic. You can do nothing but strengthen your immunity."

Some people have mocked and made a fool of us for it. However, the doctors' way of thinking is now changing and becoming similar to ours. They mean to say, "You won't be cured of the coronavirus even if you come to us. There will only be more infections. The whole country is getting infected, so please try to fight the virus using your immunity." Infected people are being quarantined in hotels, not clinics. Some are being told to stay at home.

Therefore, the only way for you to deal with the coronavirus is to strengthen your immunity. As I mentioned earlier, the mortality rate is only a small percentage. Even if it were to rise, it is not likely to go above 20 percent. If you were unable to develop immunity to the virus and were to get infected repeatedly, for a second and third time—in other words, if you got a fever—you should refrain from strenuous activities, take proper nutrition, and rest well. You might recover but without developing immunity, and after a while, you will become infected again, and the mortality rate could go up. If this is the case, it might mean the infection is caused by more than one type of virus. There could be another type of virus behind it.

Due to this uncertainty, the World Health Organization (WHO) is saying they aren't sure whether people can develop immunity to the coronavirus. From what I see, I think people can recover as long as they can maintain a certain level of hygiene, except for those who are in a weak physical condition. But if you stay at home for too long, you could get physically weaker. In many cases, your physical strength drops substantially, especially about a year after retirement, so this option is very ineffective over the long term.

To tell the truth, what strengthens your immunity is your willpower and cheerfulness. It is also important to think positively and constructively, and physically, you should strengthen your muscles.

Disinfecting your body by drinking green tea or rooibos tea, and keeping good hygiene by washing your hands

It's not so difficult to disinfect your body. Now, medicines are not so effective, but catechin, included in green tea and similar drinks, can disinfect germs, so drinking green tea often is one way to disinfect your body. There is an African tea, rooibos, that fights against illness. People have been drinking this tea for a long time. It is also sold in Japan, so I sometimes drink it too, and it gives me some spiritual light. So, I believe it's a tea created by God, a tea that boosts your immunity. There used to be a time when tea served as medicine. Tea can disinfect or sanitize your mouth, throat, stomach, and intestines.

People also talk about washing your hands and gargling. It's been said that people in China rarely wash their hands after using the public restroom, so the country is unsanitary and has poor hygiene, to begin with. It's no wonder people there get sick. Japanese people certainly wash their hands before a meal. They certainly wash their hands and often wipe them with paper, which is thrown away, after they use the restroom. In the past, it was often the case that many people would share a single hand towel, but now, hand dryers or paper towels are used.

People in the West use handkerchiefs, not tissues, to blow their nose. Decades ago, when I went to New York for work, I brought back some handkerchiefs that I had bought as souvenirs. Women at the office thanked me and began to blow their nose into the handkerchiefs. Then, they put those handkerchiefs in their pockets. I thought it was dirty and unsanitary. I was shocked because Japanese people don't use handkerchiefs that way. This might be one reason many people get infected in the West. They blow their nose into their handkerchiefs and hold on to the handkerchiefs containing their nasal mucus for the rest of the day. I'm not sure if they wash the handkerchiefs later on, but this is a risky habit.

The Japanese custom regarding a meal can help prevent you from getting infected

Here is another point. Japanese people use chopsticks to eat food, so even if their hands are dirty, it's less likely for germs to be transmitted. The possibility of infection is low.

In the West when people go to a restaurant and sit at a table, they tear and eat a piece of bread with their hands, which they haven't washed. I was shocked to see that because I thought they were civilized people. It made me feel as though they were cavemen. They take a piece of bread, put some butter on it, and eat it using their hands. Because of the dry climate, their bread is usually crispier than that in Japan, which means it lasts longer, and they eat this bread by tearing it with their bare hands. I believe they are eating germs along with the bread. Further, they don't wash their hands before eating. It's not a part of their custom. Their restrooms are not as sanitary, either.

Some restaurants in the West that are influenced by Japanese culture offer hand towels. In Japan, most restaurants provide wet hand towels or packaged hand wipes, but in the West, they generally don't. Some Japanized places might offer such items, but Westerners are apt to eat without wiping their hands first. They use those hands to shake hands or hug each other. Kissing is also a daily occurrence. So, their lifestyle is prone to high infection rates.

Perhaps Japanizing is the only way (to protect yourself from an infection). People should work to maintain good hygiene. Japanese people have a culture of using chopsticks and hand wipes. Hand towels are provided as an in-flight service in Japan, but it might not be very easy to make such things popular in other countries.

Japan's sanitary culture should spread more around the world

Once, while on a flight in India, the flight attendant offered a towel to an Indian man sitting next to me, and when he wiped his face with it, it became really dirty. I was shocked. Just think about living and eating food with your bare hands when your hands and face are covered in dust and dirt. You would have all kinds of problems.

However, the infection rate of Indian people is relatively low. They might be tough because they live with germs in their daily life. I've read something funny somewhere that said, "If you want to go to India, you should start licking the bottom of your slippers one year before you go there. Then, you will be tougher against germs. Your body can endure germs." But as you might expect, I had no interest in licking the bottom of my slippers one year beforehand.

When I went on my overseas missionary tours, I was just fine, but about half, the staff members in sections other than the secretarial division came down with a stomachache or diarrhea. They said that when they saw the housekeepers at the hotel using the same cloth to wipe cups that they had used to wipe other surfaces, without washing it, they could not drink the water there.

There is very little concept of hygiene in India. It is a country that is known for the idea that "one meter down the Ganges, the water turns holy." The ashes from cremated bodies are flushed down the river, and downstream, people are bathing and washing their face. They lack the concept of hygiene, to begin with.

If their survival rate is high, it might mean they have developed resistance to germs by living with them in their daily life. It must be noted, however, that the more civilized you become, the weaker you are apt to become against germs. Many Japanese toilets have a disinfection function on them. So, it depends on how you think.

In Japan, there was already a sewer system in place by the Edo period (1603–1868). It's astonishing that megacity Edo during the Edo period had a sewer system. In Europe, people used to go behind the bushes when nature called, which might be the reason the Black Death was rampant there. Japan, on the other hand, has been blessed with water, so it was convenient for people. I think it is good that Japan is sanitary. The Japanese sanitary culture should spread further around the world.

There isn't much need for masks in non-crowded places

To tell the truth, only a few people need to wear masks. You should wear a mask where several people are coughing due to a cold or influenza, or when you are riding in a packed train with such people. However, a mere cloth mask with its many air holes won't be able to keep you away from the coronavirus. If you are infected, your coughs will spray your droplets, so you should wear a mask to prevent that. There isn't much need for masks in non-crowded places. But if you are actually coughing or sneezing and are aware that you might be infected, you should wear a mask.

Other than that, just maintain good hygiene such as by washing your hands. Then, you won't need to worry so much. The ripple effect from the fear of the coronavirus has a larger influence.

4

Don't Be Afraid to Work

"Closed country" policies will invite serious repercussions

The Japanese government is tightening regulations. That might have been OK, but we were planning to hold an event in Shikoku at the end of April. We were scheduled to hold an event at our own El Cantare Seitankan (one of the main temples) since some people would criticize us if we held one at a public venue.

It would be nice, spring weather at the time, and I thought nothing of the coronavirus, so I was planning to see my mother and then sightsee in the Iya Valley after giving a lecture at the Seitankan. It's not often for me to be able to go to Iya. Plus, I haven't stayed in Iya before, so we made a reservation at a hotel there. I thought, "It must not be too busy in Iya, so it would be nice if I could spend a night there and go see the fresh, green leaves the next day."

Unfortunately, the hotel called us back later to decline our reservation. The caller told us, "We cannot accept reservations from visitors who come from areas that have declared a state of emergency." Simply put, the hotel was declining reservations from visitors who come from such areas because they could possibly bring the virus. The accommodation facilities in the area were all closed, so they couldn't let "outsiders" stay.

Tokushima Prefecture is doing quite well. The number of infected people has been constant at three (as of April 20), and two out of the three have already recovered. So, if the remaining one person is locked up in a "capsule" somewhere, the number would be zero.

Iwate Prefecture has had zero infected since the beginning, so it could be a great tourist destination, but I guess it doesn't want people from all over Japan to come to Iwate to sightsee. The prefecture might want to reject people who try to go there for sightseeing, but it will suffer serious repercussions later on. People won't want to go there when it wants to rebuild its tourism industry again. This could happen if it continues to conduct such "closed country" policies.

The government won't save you

For now, the coronavirus isn't causing any more damage than influenza does at its prime, so you don't need to worry as much as that hotel did. Especially, those of you who run your own business should work hard to continue doing what you are doing now, otherwise, you will really be forced to close or go bankrupt. And the government won't save you, either. They cannot get you a job. What they can do is give you rations. They can assign and distribute things like bread, milk, and rice, or regulate prices, but they cannot create jobs at will. It could be over for you if you give up, so you should do what you can, as far as possible.

If you are so worried that you will be infected by gathering in groups, you should just take the Happy Science *Kigan*, "Prayer for Defeating the Infection of Novel Coronavirus Originated in China" and receive the prayer charm. Take that prayer charm and paste it on your entrance or door, as if to say, "We've already purified this space, so it's OK."

If you are planning to hold a wedding, you should go ahead with it because postponing it won't do you any good. If you are worried, you can hold one at a Happy Science local branch or *shoja* (temple). Now, there might not be many places that offer rental space to hold a wedding, but if you can find one, another option would be to have one of our lecturers recite "Prayer for Defeating the Infection of Novel Coronavirus Originated in China" at the start and end of the wedding. The wedding itself can run as usual. I don't think you will be infected.

In Japan, it's quite difficult to hold a wedding on a *taian* (the luckiest day of the six-day cycles of the Japanese calendar), but quite easy and cheap to hold one on a *butsumetsu* (the unluckiest day). Recently, every day seems like a *butsumetsu*, so people haven't been holding many weddings, which means it should be easier for you to hold one. At this time, you can easily reserve large-scale facilities such as the Tokyo Dome and soccer fields. I would like to give lectures there if they would allow me to use those places freely. However, I'm not the only one who cannot use them. This is absolutely absurd. Anyway, you shouldn't be too afraid of getting infected by the virus.

Stay strong, both mentally and physically

Nowadays, people believe in "medical legends." They think doctors can cure diseases as if by using magic, but the ongoing infection is not something they can cure. For example, there are many things you are deceived by regarding the flu. Many of you receive flu shots every year, but the vaccine is based on the flu virus of the previous year, so it doesn't match the flu virus going around at the time. Therefore, it's not as effective.

The point is, you are paying for your painful flu shots just to reassure yourself that you are safely vaccinated and for your mental health. The reality is, the same goes for other diseases—there is no effective vaccine. That is why doctors cannot cure the coronavirus. To deal with things doctors cannot cure, you must strengthen your immunity and faith, and do what you feel you have to do. That is the only way. And, as you do so, you should think, "If my work ends with me dying, meaning, if my time is up, that is fine." Then, you probably won't come down with the coronavirus.

I do not get the flu at all. I don't. I never get it, and I don't think I ever will. There are countless flu viruses, but I don't get the flu. I didn't get it when I was working for a trading house, and I don't get it now, either. I thought, "Why should I get painful flu shots if I'm not going to get the flu?" So, I stopped receiving flu shots. A flu shot won't prevent you from getting the flu, anyway.

After all, if you are physically fit enough to repel viruses, you can blow them away. Viruses gather mainly around weak people. They feed off weaker people and kill them. That is how viruses work. Nature works in the same way. Wolves mostly prey on the weak or young sheep and goats. In the same way, viruses come to the weaker people in masses; they don't usually attack the strong. So, it's important to stay strong, both mentally and physically.

Regulations should be eased

Officials of the spring sumo tournament said that they will cancel the tournament if there is even a single person infected, but this is simply ridiculous. They should just have the person infected stay out of the tournament. There is no need for the whole tournament to be canceled.

I believe the state of emergency will be extended beyond May 6. Now, even places with zero or three cases of infection are under a state of emergency, but this has gone far enough. Regulations should be eased. Japanese people are not as active as Americans in protesting against stay-at-home orders or filing class-action lawsuits against China. They are apt to endure in silence. Even so, do what you feel you have to do.

As for food service, many places are closed for now, but those that use heat to cook shouldn't worry too much and instead open for business because viruses die when they are heated. I don't understand why those places need to close. Places that are open have been following what the government has been telling everyone to do, such as reducing the number of seats and providing more space between them. Such places might also be providing better air circulation and other things. But you will die when your time comes, so you might as well accept this.

To tell the truth, liquor with more than a certain percentage of alcohol can act as a disinfectant. I won't recommend it too much because a lot of people would get drunk, but in reality, places that offer alcohol don't need to close. They just need to tell people to drink something with higher alcohol content. When they drink it, the alcohol will disinfect their mouth and throat by killing the virus. However, this is a little inappropriate, so I won't say any more.

What you should do while you stay at home

In any case, both the central government and local public offices propose policies without much thought, so if you can somehow manage on your own, you should come up with a way to survive.

Also, although you should take care of your body, you will ultimately die at the end of the Four Pains, namely, "birth, aging, illness, and death," so you should try to live a life with which you are satisfied and without unfinished business.

If you are lawfully abiding by the government's request to stay indoors, please increase your productivity by stocking up on different things, such as preparing for what you might need later on or studying something you usually cannot. For example, you could read up on classic literature that you usually have no time to read or gain new knowledge that you will need to use later in your work. Now is the time to prepare your weapons for the next step, so you should read books or cultivate yourself.

You should refrain from watching or reading the same kind of news on different TV stations or newspapers. Instead, you should use your time for something that will help you later on, as I said above.

5

Aim to Survive through Religious Power

Happy Science music and movies keep you away from spiritual disturbances and viral infections

We have been publishing many CDs at Happy Science. The lyrics and music I compose all come from the heavenly world, so these tunes include the vibrations of the heavenly world. Therefore, you can attune your spiritual body with the heavenly vibrations just by playing and listening to these CDs.

To tell the truth, Happy Science has released the CDs "Ryuho Okawa's All-Time Best I, II, and III," so if you are running a shop such as a café, you should play these CDs. These are effective enough to keep you away from spiritual disturbances and viral infections. You can play them in your car, too. Viruses will flee, so you won't get infected so easily.

You can also play the CD of "The True Words Spoken By Buddha" (the basic sutra of Happy Science), although non-members might not be able to listen to it for long because they might go crazy. But if you are asked desperately to get rid of the virus, you can use anything we publish, since it's just like sending the lost spirits back to heaven. Our *Kigan*, sutras, and music are all effective.

Moreover, we have been making many movies as well. Quite a lot of movie theaters are closed now, which worries me, but theaters that are not so busy should play all of our movies. All they need to do is to ask customers to maintain a certain distance between each other and watch Happy Science movies. This will be good for both the theaters and the customers; everyone can watch movies without getting too close to each other.

Many movies that were scheduled for release are being canceled, so they might as well play Happy Science movies instead. If you are being told not to go to work, you should watch our movies instead. I'm sure they will be really effective.

Imagine that you are purifying the path you walk

Anyhow, the theme of this chapter is about "how good people can survive." It is about "how people living with faith and trying to serve the world can survive." Those who think the opposite most likely are attached to their physical lives, are afraid of getting infected and are seeing others around them as evil. They probably think that society is full of demon-like people who are trying to kill them. Perhaps they don't believe in devils, either. Whatever the case, they are viewing society as a group of evil people.

Such people will probably demand money from the government or say that this world isn't right and commit suicide or die after their workplace goes under. But I want to keep lost spirits to a minimum, so please don't think that there are transparent "coronavirus bombs" falling from the sky every day, as Prime Minister Abe daydreams. Rather, please imagine that you are purifying the path you walk, that the coronavirus flees and a path opens as you walk through it. Imagination really has such an effect. Please believe this.

You should have the right faith and spread the Truth

Recently, we have been hearing often about cases of domestic violence, since families are locked up at home.

This is quite understandable. Schools are empty, and they should be looking after young children, but they aren't, which leads to small afterschool facilities looking after them. But now, because such facilities fear infection, the children are gathering at tiny parks, and adults sometimes gather there as well, so those parks become crowded.

What is more, people are encouraged to stay healthy by walking or running, so quite a lot of people do that in the afternoon or early evening on Sundays. In areas of Tokyo where many foreigners live, I often see people wearing masks as they run. Sometimes, I see a group of them walking like zombies. It feels quite odd and strange, in a sense.

At any rate, try to restore things to the way they were, as much as possible. It's unfortunate that we cannot hold large-scale events at outside venues, but Happy Science staff members have been working as usual, so please try to do what you can. If you have extra time, you should study the Truth and other things and stock up on your knowledge, so that you will have resources for "future battles."

I have been recording lectures and spiritual messages, and proofreading manuscripts to get them published as books. I'm making progress on my work every day. It's at a time like this that we need to stock up a lot on our resources for future battles. That is why I'm making them. Everything published by Happy Science is effective, whether it is a picture book or a song.

I must be careful when I say this because some people might think we are doing this for a bad purpose, but you should "disinfect" the world based on the right faith and by spreading the Truth in the right way.

Regarding economic measures, don't trust what the central government or local office says too much. They might give you money, which is not bad, but even if they don't, you should think of ways to survive on your own, such as how you work, how you advertise, and other things.

Happy Science publications on the coronavirus match public demand

I saw the five-column ad for our books in the first few pages of this morning's *Asahi Shimbun* newspaper. The ad was for our recently published book *What Will Become of Coronavirus Pandemic?: Readings by Edgar Cayce* and the repeatedly printed *Spiritual Reading of Novel Coronavirus Infection Originated in China: Closing in on the real cause of the global outbreak*, even though space beings appear in the latter. This was the first time that *Asahi* had published an ad for this book. *Asahi* probably thought that people would be interested and buy these books since the novel coronavirus has infected people everywhere, so they published an ad for our books.

This is no surprise, as TV stations stream coronavirus-related news every single day. It's good if people are beginning to think, "Of course, even a religion will eventually publish a book and an ad, assuming there is freedom of speech and freedom of religion."

What Will Become of Coronavirus Pandemic?: Readings by Edgar Cayce (Tokyo: HS Press, 2020)

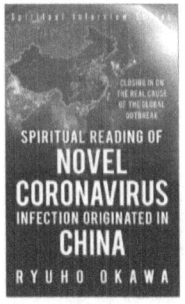

Spiritual Reading of Novel Coronavirus Infection Originated in China: Closing in on the real cause of the global outbreak (Tokyo: HS Press, 2020)

Happy Science Kigan is an "unknown attack" against viruses

The other day, *The New York Times* (NYT), which works with *Asahi Shimbun*, published a one-page article on Happy Science. It was cynical, as expected. Here's what happened. The energetic Happy Science New York Local Temple members gathered in the nearly empty Times Square and performed the "El Cantare Fight" (a sacred rite to exorcise evil spirits). This is something we would be a little worried about, too. But since there was no one around to see it, the members recorded their activity and posted it on YouTube. Then, the NYT writer found it and wrote an article on it.

I am not confident enough to guarantee that their El Cantare Fight is effective enough to wipe out the novel coronavirus in New York City. The NYT probably isn't denying this completely but wanted to ask if "immunity by faith" can really drive away the coronavirus.

Many people are indeed dying from the coronavirus, so if you can drive away the virus using such means, it's a good thing. However, it seemed that the article said that it's not right to charge a "fee" for *Kigan*, but they have no right to say that because it costs money to go to the doctor and to buy the NYT, too. And, the Happy Science lecturers performing El Cantare Fight in an empty area receive a stipend, so we need to ask for some donations. The Happy Science International Headquarters would go bankrupt if there were no donations, so we must work harder in our activities.

Such donations are small compared to your life. If you believe, you will be cured. If you don't believe, you might not be cured. But the *Kigan* effectively cured someone who didn't believe. A non-member in the U.S., whose sibling was a member in Japan, was infected with the coronavirus. After the Japanese member took the *Kigan*, the "Prayer for Defeating the Infection of Novel Coronavirus Originated in China," the person, who previously tested positive for the coronavirus, tested negative. I guess it works better than I thought.

Prayers are always heard. Viruses are busy replicating themselves, but they suddenly feel the light coming in. This is an "unknown attack" for them, so some of them will flee. They will move to another person's body since it's more comfortable there. Therefore, prayers and *Kigan* are effective. I believe it works similarly to Ultraman's

"Specium Ray,"[2] so please use it. In this way, humans have the power they have yet to use.

I hope good-hearted people will survive by dint of religious power

In this chapter, I have spoken about "how to survive the coronavirus recession." For non-believers and those who completely believe what the "godlike" mass media say, what I say might sound odd and strange, but I know it's all true based on my 30-plus years of experience.

One of my daughters once caught measles when we took a trip into the mountains. As I reached out my hand toward her, I felt tiny beings crawl up my arm in masses. And, when I played the CD of "The True Words Spoken By Buddha," they fled. They all went away. Viruses really don't like it.

Therefore, I believe it will work. Coronavirus infections and measles are caused by viruses, after all, so they will flee. It means that viruses can at least tell whether something is unpleasant or not. If something makes them feel that they shouldn't be there, that means it's effective. So, I ask you to please survive by dint of religious power.

The central government and local offices will likely continue to come up with all kinds of restraints such as laws and regulations, but if there is something that must be said, I will give my opinion as needed.

I hope good-hearted people will survive through this somehow. Please don't fail too easily. I pray that it will be so.

CHAPTER TWO

How to Strengthen Your Immunity

Originally recorded in Japanese on February 15, 2020, in the Special Lecture Hall of Happy Science in Japan, and later translated into English.

1

This Is a Vaccine by My Spiritual Power

People with a weak immune system easily die from the novel coronavirus

Recently, I published a book titled, *Spiritual Reading of Novel Coronavirus Infection Originated in China*. At first, I wasn't sure if the newspaper companies (in Japan) would allow us to advertise the book in their papers because of its unique content. But this morning, it appeared in one of the national newspapers, *Sankei*, on about a third of a page. So, we may see it in a few other papers as well, although not all. The book contains what even the mass media do not know about, and some people may struggle to believe it.

The purpose of this lecture is not to talk about people from outer space, so I won't go into details about that side of the book. What we found in this spiritual reading was the following: the coronavirus is not *just* a virus weapon or biological weapon that was developed to kill enemies. This virus seems to have been made so that it would more easily kill specific individuals when they are infected, such as elderly people who are 80 years and over and people with a disability, long-term illness, or poor immune system.

I was astonished at this, but I think the Chinese government will not officially admit this. Although Japan is becoming an aging society, so is China. China kept its one-child policy for a long time, and its population has reached about 1.4 billion people. So, with only one child per mother and father, the number of elderly people is increasing.

People who have retired in their 50s or at around the age of 60 are receiving pensions. In the past, longevity used to be celebrated, as it was rarely seen, but nowadays, people tend to dislike it. Especially in socialistic nations, there is a strong tendency for the nation to look after its people through social welfare, so the longer its people live, the heavier the tax burden will be.

What this means is, it wouldn't be strange to find vicious individuals who would want their people to die as soon as they became eligible to receive a pension. Yet, it wouldn't look good if they killed them or caused major accidents. However, what if there were a sudden outbreak of the flu, a malicious virus, or some new type of virus and it killed a mass of people because there was no vaccination? No one would be held responsible. People would simply say something like, "A bat, a pig, or a chicken must have brought the virus from somewhere," and the cause would remain unknown.

The film *Contagion*, released in 2011 and starring Matt Damon, is about the spread of a viral infection that came from Hong Kong. This virus appeared to have jumped from bats to pigs and then to humans, killing 2.5 million people in the U.S. and gradually spreading to the whole world. Now, due to the spread of the novel coronavirus, people are finding resemblances to this film, and it is gaining renewed popularity.

Creating a religious vaccine from my spiritual power

In different forms and shapes, anything can happen.

Winter is a season in which we usually see outbreaks of the flu, for example. Many people even die or fall into a critical condition due to some other infection or the collapse of their immune system. So, in this lecture, I want to create a "repellent vaccine" or "religious vaccine" from my spiritual power that you can use, not only against the novel coronavirus but to fight against any such illnesses or conditions.

Anyone who is in need of such a vaccine or is afraid of catching the virus, becoming defeated by the virus, or struggling to recover from it—anyone like this—should watch or listen to this lecture. This lecture video will be available to watch at Happy Science local branches and shoja (temples) worldwide, so you can watch it on a DVD or listen to a CD. It will be effective. By this I mean that this lecture has a special purpose: It's not always a virus (that causes an illness); sometimes, it can be caused through spiritual possession by evil or malicious spirits.

The aim of this lecture is to give you the power to fight off anything that may be possessing you, trying to make you fall ill or die, or even anything that is trying to destroy your immune system to keep you from living for a long time.

2

Abandon Your Fear and Be Positive

A viral infection is the same as spiritual possession

So, how does a viral infection occur? It's basically the same principle as spiritual possession. Viruses themselves are tiny. However, because infection occurs by the same principle as spiritual possession, how you remove and expel it from you works in the same way.

In my case, for example, when I watch the news on TV about someone's death and it shows a photograph of that person's face, the moment I see it, sometimes his or her spirit just instantly comes to me.

The news is reporting about the virus every day, so I'm starting to get worried that viruses may soon make their way to me. I'm hoping that they won't be able to since viruses do not have wings, but as I watch the news about it every day, it's making me feel like it may come.

In this way, infection usually occurs when you build some kind of a connection that enables the virus to come to you. So, please be careful.

Your fear attracts what you fear

Essentially, a viral infection passes from person to person by direct contact. You can catch it through the cough of an infected person or when you touch your face with your hands after holding onto the handrail or hand straps that an infected person has touched. It is said that humans touch their faces hundreds of times a day, so that can become a cause.

Of course, there is also an airborne infection. Many people in Hong Kong (during the demonstrations) wore masks, and some of them requested masks rather than chocolates for Valentine's Day. People in Hong Kong also fear that they could get infected through the ventilation that connects every floor via pipes in their apartments.

I just used the word "fear," but infection and fear actually have a close connection. A virus weakens the body that it's possessing, but something else happens before that. In the case of a rapid outbreak of a virus, such as the flu that is rampant every year and the novel coronavirus infection, before the virus can jump from person to person, fear spreads first.

A characteristic of fear is that it attracts what you fear, so please be aware of this. For instance, people with fear are the ones that tend to go out into crowded places. They even tend to be the first to catch the flu off a classmate when they see him or her coughing with the flu.

Why do we have fear? Fear is, of course, one of the elements in horror movies, but it is also a strong element of hell. So, when evil spirits, devils, or spirits of the dead possess people and make them fall ill or get into an accident and die, fear is often there to begin with. Fear is something that enables evil spirits to connect with you, so when you have fear, they can enter you. When you open that door or window in you, they will usually make their way in, so you need to fight your fear.

Hell is swamped with feelings of fear, but there is almost none in the heavenly world. The heavenly world is where people are living in a relaxed and comfortable manner. So, if you are the kind of person who often worries or constantly thinks of bad things, then you must be careful.

A strong tendency for this is often seen in people who study meticulously, for they are always afraid of making mistakes in their exams by answering the questions incorrectly. Bureaucratic people also worry about making mistakes. Researchers are also very meticulous. If you are the kind of person who has many worries or strong fears, you are an easy target for them (such as evil spirits), so please be aware of this.

People with an aura are difficult to be possessed

People who are difficult to be possessed are essentially individuals who emit an aura in a religious sense. It may be difficult to imagine an aura, but it is similar to the light of the halo that is shining from a Buddha statue set in a temple. The emblem that is behind me when I give lectures also symbolizes a halo. It represents golden light.

An aura is what usually emits from a person who has attained a certain level of enlightenment. However, this glow also radiates from individuals who are making an effort to attain enlightenment, individuals who live with love for the people of the world, individuals who give rather than take from others and treat them well, and individuals who live with goodwill. It glows from within these people as if they are self-generating it.

When you open your spiritual sight, you can see light shining from above the shoulders of such people or another bigger light shining from behind and over their heads.

I've mentioned this experience a few times in previous lectures, but this is what I used to do before. Back when I used to be employed, whenever I felt tired, I would go to the bathroom. If I was the only one there, I would look into the mirror and say a short prayer by calling upon the name of a specific high spirit in my mind: "So-and-so, please give me light." A pillar of light would then gently come down from above my head. I would see a cylinder of light descending from above in the reflection of the mirror. I was able to see this because I have spiritual sight, but this was how light flowed into me. I would do this whenever an evil spirit was present or I was distressed, hurt, feeling discouraged, or feeling low. The moment I filled myself with light, I would instantly feel much more positive and see a halo glowing from me. Just like a refueled car, I would come out of the bathroom feeling energized once again. This was something I used to do.

Think cheerfully, positively, affirmatively, and constructively

As I've just mentioned, one of the ways is to pray for heavenly light, but if you are still not aware of how to use the power of your mind, then the key is to change your mindset and have thoughts that are the opposite of hellish ways of thinking. Try to think cheerfully, positively, affirmatively, and constructively.

If you find yourself looking for other people's negative side and speaking ill of other people, think oppositely instead. This is important. You can, instead, try to find their strengths or think, "He may have said harsh things to me, but perhaps there is something I should learn from it. Perhaps I have to fix my way of thinking, too. Perhaps there is a reason in me as to why he said what he said." By thinking like this, you can hammer out the nail which was driven into you.

3

The Spiritual Truth behind the Virus Infection

How to recover from a viral infection is the same as expelling evil spirits

Here is my experience with a viral infection. A long time ago, when my children were small, we went to take a break up in the mountains during the summer and stayed at a log house. While we were there, one of them caught measles. It was rare, but we went to the doctors and were told it was measles.

Every time I would go near or touch my child, I would actually feel a sensation of many tiny things, something very small, crawling up my arms. They felt like very small, tiny beings. These very tiny viruses were actually alive and migrating in groups. This was when I realized how infection occurs.

In this sense, how to recover from such an illness is essentially the same as when you exorcise evil spirits—you can expel them by dint of spiritual light. This is what I experienced with measles.

A lost spirit is at the heart of a viral infection outbreak

Also, when you get the flu or even a common cold, it is said that you will get better when you pass it on to other people. It's not a nice thing to say, but there is truth in it. When severe flu or cold is going around, many clumps of tiny viruses attach onto you and possess you, but sometimes there is something at the heart of them. In the case of a very severe virus, sometimes there is a human spirit at the center of the clump, and this spirit is often a lost spirit.

Many people today die of illness. If those spirits want to bring unhappiness to this world or they want to pass their illness on to the people close to them, then those spirits could become the heart of viruses. Many viruses gather around and stick onto the spirit and form a clump. So, when the human spirit at the heart of the clump attaches to and possesses you, all the viruses also move in together in a group. I have experienced this firsthand.

Usually, when you catch a severe cold or flu, you are bedbound for about a week with a high fever. You are in bed at home or in the hospital, trying to bring down your fever. But during that time, a sick person (a possessing spirit) is inside you and suffering together with you from the fever.

Your immune system is weakened and your vitality is lowered. You lose your appetite and the energy to move. At such times, you might notice their presence inside of you. As you sweat and suffer in bed, you might sense something different and think, "Wait a minute, is this really me that is suffering right now? Or could this be someone else?" Such times are when you may actually be possessed by a spirit.

However, at times like this, when the infection is spreading far and wide, you are not necessarily possessed by close family members, such as your late parents, grandfathers, grandmothers, or siblings. It is often a random group of spirits that possess you like zombies. They possess you because they can pass on some of their suffering to you, and, at the same time, they can feel nursed and comforted through you.

Such spirits have gone without eating or drinking for a long time in the other world, so they possess living people to feel as if they are being cared for. They seek out such care. They want care from the people in this world. This is one of the reasons they possess living people.

A lot of people die in hospitals, so there's probably a huge line of such spirits. These spirits start by targeting whoever is most vulnerable to possess, so please be aware of this.

With spiritual power, you can transfer the evil spirit with the virus to others

On the contrary, if you have spiritual power like I do, and you find that something bad with many viruses has possessed you, you can transfer it in an instant to other people by saying [*while pointing to a member of the audience*], "Go to him!" Then, when you feel lighter again, all you need to do is keep your distance from him. He will then carry it for a day and has to endure it.

Of course, this is not the best way to use spiritual power, but sometimes it cannot be helped when you are busy or have urgent work and you need to recover quickly. You can transfer it to someone less busy or someone who can afford to lie in bed for a week, but please do not use this power for evil purposes. Regardless, this is possible.

4

Maintaining a Good Mental and Physical Condition

Vaccination may not be effective even if developed

This is another real-life story about my children. Every year, our family used to get flu shots. At one time, one of my children had received a shot in December but came down with a high fever in January. When the doctor gave a diagnosis and said it was the flu, we complained to the doctor and said, "That's a scam. We received flu shots just a while ago, so why the flu already?"

The doctor then told us something like, "Well, the virus that is used to make the vaccination is from the flu of the previous year, so the vaccination can protect you from last year's virus, but not this year's virus. A vaccination for the flu that is going around now will be developed next year."

We then said, "Isn't that cheating? What's the point of getting a vaccination that doesn't work?" to which he replied, "It works on some people," and also, "When the virus strain is completely different, it won't work." He kept making all kinds of excuses.

Of course, the virus strain will be different every year. But ever since I heard that, I have stopped getting flu shots. I feel there's no point in getting vaccinated if they are made for the flu strain from the year before.

I have never had the flu, but my doctor always made me have the shot. Now that I know it doesn't work, I don't see the point in going through the pain of the shot and getting one, so I don't do it anymore. So, as long as the vaccine is based on the flu of the year before, it won't work.

The vaccine for the novel coronavirus is still being developed and is said to take at least six months to a few years to complete. By the time it is made, I think almost everyone will have gotten infected already, and we will be in a situation where the vaccine will only be useful if the same virus strain spreads again.

Quit eating unhealthily, and have a healthy, balanced diet

In this way, a vaccine may work to some extent if it is developed, but if it doesn't work, you should try taking the typical precautionary measures.

First, low physical stamina and a weak mental state are major factors of infection, so it is important to start by keeping yourself in good physical and mental condition. This can be done by eating healthily, with balanced nutrients. Some people eat an unbalanced diet, for example, by forcing themselves to eat only vegetables or meat to sculpt their bodies or make themselves look good. I'm not sure how it is now, but there used to be a trend where people would only eat meat and avoid carbohydrates or sugar to shape their bodies. From the beginning, I used to think that such a diet was dangerous for the body, and, sure enough, people have slowly begun noticing it, too. There are nutrients that you cannot get in meat. Your brain gets energy from glucose only. Glucose acts like fuel for the brain, so without it, you cannot use your brain to study, read books, or work. Meat alone will not do the job.

So, you will either need to have sugar by itself or via carbohydrates. When you do, your body will break it down into glucose and send the nutrients to your brain. Given this, you should refrain from eating an extreme diet. You may see people building their muscles by eating only meat, but that is a little dangerous for the body. If your work requires you to do only physical labor, then it may be fine for you, but if it also requires your brain, then you will become glucose deficient. At the time, your body will start breaking down the glucose stored in your body, but as soon as it runs out of stock, your body will get weaker and weaker.

If you decide to eat only vegetables, that will make you protein deficient. Of course, there are animals such as cows and rabbits that can develop their body by eating only grass, but humans are not made in the same way. Humans are made to be omnivores, so I recommend that you take the nutrients that your body needs.

5

Spiritual Causes of Allergies and Ways to Overcome Them

An example of recovery from an allergy through self-reflection

This story may not be directly associated with this lecture, but this is what one of our female singers from our talent agency who sings a Happy Science song experienced.

She recently had an opportunity to sing a cover for one of our songs. As she felt that she needed to be in tune with angels, draw in the light from the heavenly world, and fill herself with light, she made an effort to do self-reflection to purify her mind as she practiced singing. Afterward, she realized that the egg allergy that she had been suffering from for a long time was completely cured.

Her symptoms used to be so extreme that she would get an allergic reaction as soon as she would eat or touch a little bit of egg. She is a young lady, but her allergy was suddenly, completely cured. So, we can even cure serious allergies. In cases like these, spiritual possession could be the reason for allergic reactions.

Allergic reactions can arise from fearful experiences from your past lives

Allergic reactions could also surface due to past-life experiences. If you have had a very unpleasant or fearful experience in a past life, when you come across a similar situation in this life again, as if you are having déjà vu, then the same fear can come back to you again.

For example, some people are very scared of water. They fear a river, a canyon, or a lake. This is often because these people drowned in their past life. Others are scared of fire. When people have died in a fire in a past life, such an experience will leave a deep scar on their soul, so they feel frightened when they see a fire. Yet other people are scared of all kinds of birds, or even chicken meat. These people may have been involved in some bird-related incidents.

If you live with superstitions, your body may react to them

Back when many superstitions were going around, take the Edo Period in Japan, for example, people held to false beliefs such as you should not eat animals with four legs. So, if they had fallen ill or were persecuted for eating them in the past, then that belief could become a trigger to cause some kind of reaction.

In the Meiji Period (1868–1912), too, it was often said that horns would grow on your head if you drank cow's milk. Only 100 or 150 years ago, Japanese people truly believed that it was OK to drink human milk, but cow's milk would give you horns. It was also believed that it was dangerous to eat *sukiyaki*, a Japanese hotpot which consists of beef.

In this way, when you hold superstitions, your belief in them may develop some kind of a reaction.

This is what I learned from something I read, but there is a tribe in Africa that believes they can die from eating banana. I don't know on what basis this superstition came about, but because they are brainwashed by such ideology, they can end up fainting the moment they are told, "By the way, what you just ate had some banana in it."

Your knowledge and past-experience can be the reason for your allergic reactions

There is a religion that prohibits eating pork and a religion that prohibits eating beef. In Hinduism, a religion prevalent in India, people believe that cows are a means of transportation for the gods, so cows cannot be killed or eaten. Therefore, even if a cow is lying in the middle of the road, a car cannot run over it. In terms of Islam, in Pakistan, for example, people cannot eat pork as it is believed to be impure.

Such people will have an allergic reaction just from eating a pig or a cow. Even if he or she hadn't eaten beef, they might still have a reaction at once by simply being told that "this frying pan that was used to cook today's meal is also used to cook beef steak," or even just by hearing the word "pig" after a meal. So, it's more of a mental reaction. Some people can actually die from shock, so it can be dangerous.

I read a book written by an Iranian author the other day that said that people in Iran are also not allowed to eat pork, but when the author of the book came to Japan and tried *tonkatsu*, a Japanese pork cutlet, he said it tasted too good to keep to the precept, and he finished it all. Then, he wanted his parents to try it also, so he took them to eat it, but because he couldn't say that it was pork, he told them that it was flying squirrel when they asked him what it was. Thinking that it was a deep-fried flying squirrel, his parents also said that it tasted good and finished it all. Who knows what may have happened to them if he had told them that it was pork the moment he was asked.

In this way, our knowledge and past-experience can become a trigger for an allergic reaction or an illness due to mental breakdown and heart attacks. If a taboo or superstition has been deeply ingrained in you and you seem to react to it, please study Buddha's Truth and examine yourself based on it to stop the allergic reactions or malignant symptoms.

Animals have spirit bodies

Of course, there is a religious way of thinking that believes it is not good to eat living things. But in Buddhism, monks and nuns eat vegetables and also meat because the food that they receive from lay members when they go on their alms round can contain them both. In such cases, they will consume the meat with gratitude, but only under the condition of the threefold rule, that is, "three kinds of pure meat." For example, they are not allowed to eat any meat they are told was killed specifically for them to eat, meat of an animal that they saw being killed, or meat of an animal that was likely to have been killed as an offering to them.

Spiritually speaking, however, not only monks and nuns but all common people such as farmers also feel that way, to some extent. Anyone would feel pain if they had to slaughter a pig when the time came, especially if they had given a name to it and raised it with love. The same goes for chickens. Chickens will keep flapping their wings even if you chop their head off; it's quite frankly scary.

When I was a child, I bought a chick at a local shrine festival and raised it inside a cardboard box that I kept warm with a light bulb. But as it grew, it became difficult to raise it at home, so I took it to a friend of mine whose family owned a farm and asked them to take care of it, and it grew into an adult hen.

One day I asked him, "So, how's the hen doing?" and he replied, "Oh, we ate it." I felt sorry for it, knowing that it was eaten, and asked him how he did it, to which he replied, "It kept running around, so we held it down by its neck and chopped its head off with a hatchet. Its blood spilled everywhere, and it still kept flapping its wings even without its head." Out of shock, I asked, "Wow... and how were you able to eat it?" to which he replied, "Well, we farmers have to get used to it to make a living." Even so, it's not easy to eat animals that you have raised yourself.

I remember in *Peter Rabbit*, there is a scary story about a rabbit being turned into a pie. My children owned rabbits then, so when I imagined them being made into a pie, it was just too frightening, and I would not be able to do such a sad thing.

Rabbits also have spiritual bodies. From my experience, not every rabbit spirit we owned returned to me, but the spirit of the first one came and stayed around me for a week after it died. The rabbit used to sleep in a different room to mine, but for a week or so, its spirit body was hopping everywhere in my room, jumping on and off my bed. It was transparent, but I was able to tell that it was the rabbit. Its spirit body was actually hopping around and on and off my bed. So, they do have spirit bodies.

The rabbit must have stayed around because it had grown attached to us. But after about a week, in my mind, I said to it, "I think it's about time that you return to the rabbit realm in the spiritual world and are reborn again.

You should return to where you should be." Then, it left. I believe rabbits incarnate in short intervals, so it may have been reborn somewhere after about a month. This is its cycle of reincarnation.

In this way, I have had a rabbit come to me after it died.

Don't be too attached to your pets that have died

Just as depicted in *Pet Sematary*, a film about scary things that can take place if you have a pet cemetery near your home, those things can happen.

People living in urban cities nowadays give a lot of affection to their pets. We see pets that are dressed in pet clothes when they are out on walks, and some of them even eat human food. I say this is just about acceptable. In one of the cafés that allow pets that I go to, however, I sometimes see a dog at the table next to us eating with its owner. I go there with my grandchild sometimes, and when I do, I can't help but wonder which of the two is smarter, my grandchild or the dog.

If dogs are taken care of like human beings, they too will, after all, grow attached to this world, their home, and their owner after death. But since they have spirit bodies, in the case of animals, it is not good to be too attached to them after they die. They are each born with individualities, but just as how all bulldogs look similar, their range of individual diversity is very narrow and limited. So, when animals return to the other world, they become a part of a collective spiritual group. They often become one with their animal group and are reborn from there, so if you treat them too much like humans, they'll end up developing their individuality, and that will not be good for them.

Also, many people bury their pets in a cemetery, but I don't think it's good to treat them too much like humans. What I mean is, when you create such a place for them, it can cause them to grow more attached. My family also considered making a cemetery in the garden for our first pet and burying it there when it died, but we realized it was not good after all. Memorial services for pets have grown popular nowadays, but it's best to try to forget about them after some time has passed.

There is the term "pet loss," which signifies that owners suffer from losing their pets. But if you think too deeply about your pets or give them a specific place to grow attached to, they will not be able to leave this world and may start to cause spiritual disturbances. Pets especially can cause spiritual disturbances with small children, so because all things are transient, you should pray and tell your pets, "You should be reborn in another new place," and cremate them. Do not spend too much time thinking about them.

I used to have a dog that lived for about 15 years, from my elementary school to university days. I think he lived for as long as a dog can live, but after he died, his spirit kept appearing for quite some time. He died when I was a university student, but my dog would come to see me even after I had my spiritual awakening and had started to travel back and forth between this and the other world. I do not think this was in one of the higher realms, but when I would travel to a very bright and beautiful meadow, I would often see him running around, so he probably wanted to see me too. In his case, he wasn't coming to see me. We just saw each other in the spirit world, but he appeared quite often. I stopped seeing him after about 10 years, so he may have been reborn somewhere. These things happen. Of course, you can treat your pet with love and care, but when it dies, you should abandon your attachment.

People living in cities seem to overdo it for their pets. Even our rabbit experienced being hospitalized at a pet hospital before it died. It cost ¥12,000 [about US$120] per night, and I remember being surprised at how expensive it was. We kept it there because the doctors told us that it would die if we took it home. Surprisingly, they had oxygen masks and drip infusions even for rabbits. I didn't see it because I wasn't the one who took it to the hospital, but we were charged ¥12,000 for one night. It may not be much different from the hospital fee for human beings. This is how it is in cities. Of course, you can treat your pet how you want, but once it dies, it is better to forget about it as soon as you can.

The effects of joining the events of Happy Science

In these ways, animal-related incidences and past-life experiences can affect your illness. These things are often forgotten, but if you can have a spiritual reading as to their cause, they are easy to determine because food allergies and such are often influenced by them.

If food allergies or some deformation of your body is caused by spiritual reasons or through the laws of cause and effect, then there are possibilities that they may disappear when your nature changes to a certain extent through the events, lectures, or sacred ceremonies, sacred rites, and prayers of Happy Science.

I've spoken about this before, but some people have a mark on their bodies and are struggling to remove it. The cause of this is often related to how they have died in their past life.

For example, if you were born during a period of war and were either pierced by a spear, cut by a sword, or shot by an arrow, you are likely to be born with a mark on your skin. If you find a mark that you cannot remove in a strange place on your body, it is because this mark is also on your spiritual body. After you die, the injury remains on your astral body for some time, so you may have identified it as a part of you, or you may have died slowly in agony from the pain of an arrow that struck you. In such a case, the memory that has been etched into you would appear on your skin as some mark in your next life. I haven't experimented to see if we could make such marks go away, but based on these principles, they may disappear in some cases.

Some people also develop abnormal skin problems across their bodies. For example, there is an illness known as the "fish skin" disease, where the skin on the body becomes scaly like a fish. Such symptoms have probably developed because they were fishermen in their past life, and they didn't have enough appreciation for the fish they caught. If they were the kind of fishermen who continuously kept taking fish and killed a great many, then that may have been the reason for such a symptom to develop.

The causes of such fairly abnormal cases often have spiritual reasons. I'm sorry that I can't afford to conduct personal readings for each person, but I would like you to know that many people have found that their illness has gotten better after having taken part in the spiritual practices of Happy Science, which give you heavenly light, or just by reading our books—such as the spiritual message series—so these practices are also important.

6

The Secret to Strengthen Your Immunity and Fight against Viruses

Your belief in God becomes your immunity

In regards to the infection of the novel coronavirus that has spread in 2020, there is another meaning to it, or, in other words, a political meaning, so it will spread to a certain extent.

More than 60,000 people have been infected and over 1,000 people have died (as of February 15). China has the greatest number of infected people in the world, and Japan seems to be coming second. The number is a little less in other countries, but if this spreads too much, there will be unfavorable circumstances. The infection in Japan has occurred in the Okinawa, Wakayama, and Chiba Prefectures, and an increasing number of cases have been found via unconfirmed routes. It is bad.

So, please do not have too much fear. Just like the "faith immunity" I spoke about in the book I mentioned earlier, *Spiritual Reading of Novel Coronavirus Infection Originated in China*, your power of belief in God will become your immunity. This is one reason why faith is known to cure illness from a long time ago. Because of your faith, your immunity will strengthen greatly. Real-life experiments have also proved that it actually boosts it in reality.

Your immunity will strengthen if you believe in God's power, believe in God's protection, and live by your faith. If any malicious virus or bacteria enters your body, your white blood cells will become abnormally active and fight very hard to combat evil germs and viruses that try to invade your body. Our bodies are equipped with a system where the white blood cells become stronger to combat and eat all the malignant viruses that come into our bodies.

If our bodies easily become sick when it is invaded by viruses, then people who are living in underdeveloped regions with very poor sanitation should all get sick, indeed. But in fact, many of them are completely fine. That is because we all have what it takes to fight viruses inside our bodies.

If you live with fear or you have distanced yourself from the faith, your immunity will weaken greatly. On the other hand, if you think, "I am one of God's angels" and live in an angelic way, then your immunity will strengthen. When you live sincerely, thinking, "God, please protect me for as long as I have a mission," then your body can drive out any bad viruses that come into your body. Viruses, or any such kind of thing, move around in a large mass, but they are indeed very tiny, so you can, of course, drive them out from your body.

Meditation also has the power to fight viruses

Another way is to use the power of meditation. There is a meditation called the *Nanso no Ho* or "Golden Butter Meditation," in which golden butter envelops your whole body. It is where you imagine yourself with a block of butter on top of your head. This golden butter gradually melts and seeps into your whole body from your organs to your bone marrow, and you meditate on it. This method has been practiced by Buddhists, and it can help combat viruses.

If every day, time and time again, you meditate on the golden-butter-like being on top of your head given to you by Buddha and let it gradually melt and seep everywhere into your body, the heavenly light will go into you and defeat the virus.

Balanced nutrition and occasional exercise are also important

Other things you should be careful of are your intake of balanced nutrition and exercising and training your body occasionally at your own pace. In the case of elderly people, a light fall that breaks a bone, for example, can cause them to become bedridden. So, in this case, it is important to make efforts to check the weather forecast regularly, avoid going out on snowy days or walking on icy roads, and refrain from wearing slippery shoes. Breaking a bone or such after a fall especially makes elderly people prone to catching all kinds of illnesses, so please be careful.

I don't see myself as an old person yet, but I have anti-slip mats in my bathroom as a precautionary measure. When I give a public lecture, I sometimes stay at a hotel near the venue hall. My very adept secretaries send items via express delivery to the hotel beforehand, and one of the items is anti-slip mats. As soon as they arrive at the hotel, they set the mats everywhere, both inside and outside the bathtub—I'm sure the cleaners are surprised when they see them—but they do this because there is no promise that nothing will happen. I would feel sorry if any of my members ever had to be told, "Last night, Master arrived but slipped in the bath and hit his head."

I cannot go and see the hotel beforehand, and some bathrooms can be slippery, especially the bathrooms that are made of marble. So, it's done for extra safety. Other things we are also careful of are room temperature and humidity.

In this way, without building too much fear, you must be careful in a worldly sense. Also, it is important to be one with the power of light, or God's spiritual power, and think of it as your protective armor. This will help you to recover more easily.

A malicious pandemic spreads when there are many political issues

In Mainland China, the spread of the novel coronavirus has currently encouraged the people to demand disclosure of information and the freedom of speech. This is completely natural.

The government is trying yet again to suppress its people, and it is likely hiding the true number of affected people. We currently know the number of infected people living in and around Wuhan, but we don't hear much about the number of infected people in Beijing, for example. So, I guess they are withholding the information.

I hope that the government will take this as an opportunity to respect each life and acknowledge various ways of thinking, including the idea of considering their citizens' opinions or valuing people's lives. These are other reasons why certain viruses become pandemic.

Since long ago, whenever a plague or a bad illness has gone rampant, it is often because there is a problem with the politics, so people in top governmental positions should reflect on themselves and their ways of thinking and revise what should be revised.

This pandemic is caused by a malicious virus, but a virus that "shouldn't have needed to appear" is now spreading. So, when this sort of power or mechanism that is beyond human power is at work, you should understand that it is a sign urging people to look back on their actions and to learn the importance of valuing human life and human rights.

How to Strengthen Your Immunity

Let's stay healthy and help the world prosper

I pray that this lecture will help more and more people to make an effort to become a stronger person. Another very important thing I'd like to mention is keeping the right faith and thinking, "I want to stay healthy and help the world prosper." This is one way to keep in good health and prevent yourself from developing dementia after middle age and to maintain a sharp, fully functioning brain. Fear is not good to have, and too much self-pity will draw bad things to you, so you should keep them to a minimum.

In this lecture, I have spoken on a topic that you can use on various occasions by reading it repeatedly every year, so please come back to it. You can also listen to the CD or watch the DVD.

Some people may not be able to accept this lecture content on how to strengthen your immunity. Even so, if their family members or people around them know about it and believe in it, then that itself will have an effect. If the family or people around them think, "Oh, maybe this is his problem," or "Oh, this could be where she can make improvements," then, in a spiritual sense, the viruses or the spirits possessing him or her will be besieged by goodwill.

So, the spiritual power against the illness will gradually become stronger, and it will be "out with the demons, in with good fortune." In this way, the more people who know the content of this lecture, the better it will be.

CHAPTER THREE

Current View on the Coronavirus Infection

*Q&A Session on the Lecture,
"My Philosophy of Life"*

*Originally recorded in Japanese on May 2, 2020,
in the Special Lecture Hall of Happy Science in Japan,
and later translated into English.*

1

Coronavirus Is No Different Than the Flu

> **QUESTION:**
> Currently (May 2), the novel coronavirus infection that originated in China is causing big problems worldwide. To combat this issue, there is a strong wave in Japan surrounding the notion of "Stay Home," which is telling people that "doing nothing is right and breaking this rule is evil." From such a notion, which is being conveyed by some politicians and the mass media, we feel a sense of threat, as if this country is turning into a totalitarian nation.
>
> However, at the same time, you have been receiving messages from the heavenly world and are fighting by conveying important ways of thinking to change the direction of the world for the happiness of all people. Could you tell us your current opinion on the coronavirus infection?
>
> Also, you often courageously give powerful opinions that withstand the tide of this day and age, like in the case of this coronavirus problem. To the extent that you can, could you also tell us the process that you take when you draw a conclusion on how to lead us?

Comparing various opinions until a conclusion is found

ANSWER:
I have published many spiritual messages on the novel coronavirus. I didn't make any predictions as to how much this virus would spread and how many deaths there would be beforehand. We realized that the number of infections and deaths would be very large when we recorded spiritual messages from various spirits. Of course, I was worried whether people would accept this and whether people would think that Happy Science was just inciting fear in people. Regardless, I collected much information and various opinions and compared them until I reached a conclusion. This is how I usually work.

This is a method I acquired during my law-degree days. Of course, there are laws, but we cannot simply enter the details in the computer and make judgments on the cases. This applies when judgments are made regarding criminal actions committed by people in this world, or in civil actions that deal with monetary problems between people. It doesn't always work that way. We are taught to consider and weigh the opinions of concerned individuals until we reach an appropriate conclusion. That is the kind of study law requires, and I still have the habit.

Politicians do exactly as they are told by some epidemiologists

In politics, there is a diversity of values. There is no particular way of thinking that will always give you an answer, so politicians have to clash with one another and choose an answer. If one side has 100 points while the other has zero points, then there's nothing to consider since the answer is already there; but, that is not often the case.

For example, in the context of the coronavirus, the government (as a whole) and the governors (of the various prefectures) each found themselves an epidemiologist to act as an advisor and simply reported what they were told. Epidemiologists have a closed knowledge system in the field of medicine, and they sometimes have narrow views. If they had had several chances to experience an infection during their time at work, they could learn how much of an impact their opinion has based on their experiences. But oftentimes, infection would be new to the epidemiologist.

What I mean to say is that it is highly likely that these epidemiologists cannot view things from the perspective of other fields or a comprehensive perspective. These people are prone to fall into the so-called "expertise trap."[3]

Politicians are good at escaping from responsibility. They would hand their responsibility over to experts by quoting their opinions and making it look as if they themselves have no responsibility.

An epidemiologist who maintains that infectious disease does not actually exist

An epidemiologist who boarded the cruise ship containing coronavirus-infected patients that had parked up at the port in Yokohama, Japan, and actually saw the situation said in one of his books, "Infectious disease does not actually exist." It sounded as if he was denying his own occupation, but he said, "Infection is just a phenomenon and not an illness. It is a phenomenon in that many people show certain symptoms, but it is not an illness." He also said that due to the reports by the mass media, people think that an illness called the novel coronavirus infection is spreading, but it is not true. To a certain extent, I agree with what he said.

Is there a need to be this cautious of the coronavirus?

Coronavirus does exist if you look under a microscope. But viruses are actually everywhere. At times, they can attach to people and make them fall ill, while at other times, they are just repelled. In most cases, people can repel them.

When the virus enters the body, it multiplies, and it reaches the lungs through the bronchial tubes. It can often kill people who already have other illnesses or the elderly.

However, viruses themselves are actually very primitive beings, but we may not be able to call them living organisms or life forms. They are extremely tiny beings, and they do not have systems that living organisms have. They have no mouth, no eyes, or no ears; they have neither a stomach nor intestines. They contain a very small amount of RNA or DNA inside their tiny protein, so a single virus itself may not be fit to be called a living organism. They are midway between a non-living object and a living organism.

When they are a good match with the body that they enter, they will keep on multiplying, and the person will fall ill and die if the virus goes into their lungs and collapses the organ; but the basic function of the virus alone is actually not very different from that of regular flu and colds.

Just as the Party Leader of the Happiness Realization Party, Ryoko Shaku, has already said, about 10,000 people die from the flu every year, and it is normal. So the question is whether it is right to be excessively defensive over the coronavirus, more so than over the flu, when it has only caused a few hundred deaths. When a school decides to close due to the spread of the flu, other schools that are not affected would usually remain open as usual. Neither would all the shops and department stores close because of the flu that is going around.

In the case of hospitals, the mass media has been reporting that they are having a medical-care breakdown as if it were the name of an illness. That is what the mass media named it. They first said it was a medical-care breakdown phenomenon, and then, later on, they called it a "supermarket breakdown." They are professionals at giving things a name and making it a trend, so it cannot be helped. But in actual fact, it appears to me that the hospitals are just having trouble because many people are being brought in even when there is no particular treatment available. Of course, they can offer respiratory support to people who are having breathing difficulties or help those who need nutritional support.

Either way, the government is now even trying to disseminate a "fake medicine." Due to there being no vaccination, they are trying to popularize a medicine that is used to treat other illnesses in the hope that it will be effective to some degree, but that will not fundamentally solve this problem.

The novel coronavirus should be weak against sunlight and fresh air

Seeing how this virus, which stems from bats and which humans should not normally catch, is the cause of the novel coronavirus infection, I'm thinking that to make it easier for human beings to catch it, this virus was cultivated in animals that live near humans and can transfer illness to humans. This is very likely to be the case, and I'm guessing that it was biologically made.

I also guess that, because this is a bat virus, the virus must dislike places that bats themselves usually dislike. We are told to stay at home, but bats live inside caves, so I

Current View on the Coronavirus Infection

strongly think that we should be doing the opposite. The virus should be weak against sunlight and fresh air.

Japan is the only country that is telling people to avoid *San-Mitsu*, the three C's.[4] We hear people around the world talk about social distancing, but it is only Japan that is talking about San-Mitsu in a way that makes me think that esoteric Buddhists will get angry (because San-Mitsu is the same pronunciation as one of the esoteric Buddhist terms). I believe this concept is what the epidemiologists came up with, but what it is trying to say is, "You will not catch the virus if you do not gather in groups and avoid close contact."

I just cannot help asking, "Is this really the opinion of experts?" Everyone has that level of knowledge. Of course, no one would get infected if everyone lived alone on separate islands. This is simple knowledge, and I want to tell them, "If you are an expert, please give us a more expert-like opinion. You should tell us how people can be cured." If they cannot say this, then they are not experts and can think nothing more than normal people. What epidemiologists do is research viruses and other things along those lines. They do not develop ways for us to stop a virus from spreading when the phenomenon actually happens.

2

Protect Yourself

Do not depend on the government

If vaccination is developed, it may be somewhat effective, but we already know that will not be any time soon. All the damage that societies around the world are now facing appears to me to be a kind of pathological condition, so there are various ways to fight against it.

As for me, since I have studied fields such as management and financial affairs, I can understand the situation better—more so than the mass media. I knew straight away that the subsidies from the government would not be enough to cover the damages. A nation cannot forever support its citizens who have quit their jobs. This is the same as acknowledging that parents cannot take care of their unemployed children forever.

Rather (in the case of the Japanese government), they want taxes from the people, and that is why they raised the tax rate. So it's a lie when they say that they will take care of their people if they quit their jobs. It's impossible for them to take care of them. If they did so, we would have to pay the price.

At such a time, I always consider the "batting average." In the case of the coronavirus, I would logically judge the gains and losses after I had calculated how many people would be infected and die based on the world average. The leaders of the world, should, at least, think like this.

When big companies take a long break, there is no way that the government can cover their losses. If a company develops a deficit of billions of dollars, there is no way that the government can pay back the full amount. When one big company goes out of business, that itself can cause great confusion.

For example, great confusion occurred when Japan Airlines went bankrupt in the past. It took a lot of effort for the government to ask Mr. Kazuo Inamori to take on a turnaround manager. But if this happens all at once to a large number of major companies from all industries, including smaller companies, too, then there is no way that the government can help overcome it all.

So, we need to think simply and rationally to some extent. Just like in the military, there is nothing we can do but remove individuals who are seriously injured from the line of battle and send them to the medical team and encourage the uninjured to continue their job and fight.

The government appears to have kept people out of their offices; such action is, on the whole, equivalent to "killing people" in a certain sense. So, what the government should do is to look at their fiscal resources and calculate how long they can sustain the society if they tell everyone, "do nothing," "don't work," and "stay at home." They need to clarify this point. It is very irresponsible for them to tell people to do so when they don't even have the money.

In other words, there is no way that the government can help recover a company that has gone bankrupt, so you should do what you can to protect yourself.

The government can only do a negligent and sloppy job. For example, only the day before this lecture recording, only two masks, which were dubbed "Abenomasks" (Abe's masks) were delivered to the Master's sacred temple of Happy Science. I was astonished beyond words. The reason why each household got only two masks is that the mailman was supposed to drop one packet into every mailbox. From the size of the building, it should have been obvious that two masks would not be enough.

We also have dormitories that a number of our staff live in, but they, too, only got two masks dropped into the one mailbox they have. It should be obvious from the size of the buildings that more than two people are living inside. They are a three-story or a four-story building, so there are a number of people living there. When I heard this, I thought, "I see. The government didn't even check the number of people that are living in each house. They just organized a packet each to be mailed to every household, and that's their job done."

If this is the case, then the same may also happen with the subsidies distributed by the government. People who fail or cannot fill out the application form to receive the subsidy will probably be left to either die from hunger or go freelance when they lose their jobs.

Among the blind or the deaf, there are people who are acupuncturists, or moxibustion, or massage therapists. They are currently suffering from a great loss of customers. These people will struggle even more to find compensation for their losses.

Healthy people should work

In terms of hospitals, they will not be able to treat or cure patients if they have too many. The job of doctors is essentially to be defeated since every human will die one day. People will 100 percent die, so, given this, doctors have no chance of winning because it is 100 against zero. All that doctors can do is alleviate patients' symptoms for a while and enable them to live a little longer or delay their death so that they can support their family or their company during critical times.

When I was hospitalized at the age of 47, I saw the reality of how powerless they are. Hospitals couldn't do anything. If we are put on the bed, given an IV drip and a catheter, we cannot go anywhere. We will be completely tied to the bed, so we will automatically become "sick people." It is almost impossible for us to escape from the hospital with the IV drip stand, so we just become a sick person. Once we are "tied," then that is it.

In this way, hospitals essentially "tie" people to the bed, give them an IV drip, and that is all. This is what most hospitals do, and right now, they have lines of hospital beds even in the aisles. If, when looking at this condition, you think that "medicine is almighty," then I think that is wrong.

Sometimes, we need to sacrifice something small to save something bigger. What we should do is to think about how we can make sure that the majority of the population can continue taking care of their family next year and beyond. Of course, people who are in critical condition should be protected by society. But just as not every classmate will catch a cold from a sick classmate, those of you who feel completely fine or can say, "I don't have the flu, neither do I have a temperature," should work. This is what I want to tell you.

Think from various angles

I have made such judgments many times already; in most cases, I try to gather a wide variety of information and knowledge sources to avoid becoming a person with a narrow field of expertise and make judgments from various angles. I make such worldly efforts while I gather information from the guiding spirits of the higher dimensions about how they see the situation. Then I weigh all the information and make my own conclusion as to what we should do.

Sometimes, what the higher spirits say is not suitable for this current day and age, and if that's the case, I do not follow everything that they say. As a result, our opinions sometimes do not match. There are judgments we can make because we have acquired knowledge in this world. This is the process that I take when I give my opinion.

Make your own judgments of your own problems

Just like with the "Abenomask policy" I mentioned earlier, the government is made up of people who think that their job is done by sending out only two masks to a place the size of the Master's sacred temple with a decent number of people living inside. So it is very unlikely that they can anticipate what will happen and make the right move. This level of ability is below average for a normal company, but this is the norm for bureaucratic jobs.

When a problem arises unexpectedly, what they do is to try to avoid being criticized by the mass media, and because Soka Gakkai and Komeito insisted, they disseminated ¥100,000 [about US$1,000] to every citizen, and that was it. Soka Gakkai has founded their political party and started participating in the election campaigns, so they want achievements. Because they are getting ¥100,000, their members can use that to fund their election activities. As they see it, a good job has been done. So, they can say to their members, "Your support of the election campaigns has returned to you as money." Even so, we don't know if this ¥100,000, handed out to every citizen, from babies to the elderly, in Japan, can actually solve the problems of people other than their members. In terms of this fund, many people will not be able to get the money because most people are likely to be too lazy to even fill out the application form and apply for it properly. What's more, this policy may have been a show, with this taken into consideration.

Also, the Tokyo government has been requesting places like hair and beauty salons to close their shops because there is a high risk of getting infected. They have been saying that they will fund from ¥150,000 to ¥300,000 [about US$1,500 – 3,000] to shops that voluntarily close during the long weekends. But funding ¥150,000 to ¥300,000 is very likely to only cover the amount of one person's monthly salary that beauty and hair salons in Tokyo pay their staff. They also need money to pay for other things, like rent, but this expense will not be covered. So, if this continues for a few months, there is certainly a risk of them going bankrupt.

So, even if the Governor of Tokyo, Yuriko Koike, has announced funding of ¥150,000 to ¥300,000, until we know when the payment will be made, for how long they will fund you, and when this funding will end, we have to protect ourselves. If you naively follow what the government says, you may not have enough money, for example, to cover your children's school fees by next year. This is what I'm trying to say. On top of this, there may be family disputes that may lead to divorce.

The government has a fixed way of doing the job that they use on everybody. But every person's circumstances are different, so we each have to make our own judgments.

3

The Qualities Expected of a Leader

The government should not do things that discourage people from helping each other

There is another bad point that I want to highlight. Many of the local governments might want to ask the central government to declare a state of emergency, but you must have received aid from people around the country when typhoons hit your area.

For instance, at the time of the earthquake that hit Kobe City, people across the nation helped you by sending relief goods. When the Great East Japan Earthquake struck northeastern Japan, people from all over the country helped you. The people of Tokyo helped save power by reducing their electricity use by half the usual amount.

Despite all that, Japanese governors are telling people not to come to their localities, after seeing the numbers of infected people in urban areas. I felt a little sad about this. The cameras showed people saying, "Don't come here during the long weekends," or people holding signs that said, "Don't come," or "Don't come to Shizuoka Prefecture." But this will divide the nation, and people will grow sick of each other.

Iwate Prefecture is yet to see an infected person, but if the people there equip themselves with swords and spears to keep out a single person as if to say, "We will never let a single person enter the holy land of Iwate," then things will go wrong in Japan. In Iwate, there was a situation in which a returning pregnant woman, who had gone into labor, was not accepted by some of the hospitals there because she would have to be quarantined for two weeks due to testing. But this was a little inhumane.

In Tokushima Prefecture, there have only been five infected people (as of May 2), but when we tried to invite people from the Shikoku region (consisting of four prefectures) for our event, the locals watched and made anonymous reports of cars with license plates from other prefectures because those places have many infected people. People coming from those areas were harassed; their cars were marked with paint or the surfaces were scratched. At the same time, however, some people wrote to the local newspaper saying visitors should not be harassed like that. There was such a conflict going on.

Current View on the Coronavirus Infection

A prefectural governor is saying that people should never visit his prefecture during the long weekends, but this will invite problems later on. Take the Izu area in Shizuoka Prefecture, for example, which is about to go under because fewer customers are visiting there. A resort area like Izu has a hard time unless people visit during the Golden Week holidays; however, if the Shizuoka governor says not to come or not to leave the station, people will not want to go there.

It's bad for a wall of hatred to exist between visitors and locals. Rather, what he should say is something like this: "Thank you very much for helping us every year. Unfortunately, our measures against the infection are still inadequate, so please stay at home if your schedule allows. If you have already had something planned, please take appropriate measures to prevent infections." He should use adequate expressions. But if he restricts anyone and everyone or tries to make people feel indebted by saying, "It's better than being in a lockdown," they will not be happy with him.

Many natural disasters are yet to come, so you shouldn't try to do things that discourage people from helping each other.

The government should come up with places that people can go

When Ms. Koike, who is now the Tokyo governor, formed her new party, she used the word "exclusion," and her popularity dropped quite a lot. What she is saying now also seems like the principle of exclusion.

Now, some shops are open for business, even if those around them give them a cold look, but those other shops sometimes criticize by saying that the open ones are trying to make money by opening their stores while everywhere else is closed, or they tell the mass media to report on the shops that are open and to stress that they should close their shops.

However, I believe this is wrong. People may be allowed to take a walk outside, but they do not know what to do because many of them have nowhere to go. So, the government must come up with a place where people can go. Sure, the government needs to ask people to be careful not to get infected, but this is also what they need to do.

As you can see, Happy Science has been making efforts to tell people which direction will be the best option for them, by looking at things from multiple perspectives and eventually adding the power gained from our experiences and past judgments.

Happy Science conducted spiritual readings to determine the identity of the coronavirus. This virus has many unknown aspects in the worldly sense, so I thought I should cooperate. Since no one else can do this, some people might think we are forcing our dogma upon them, but we have published these books because we thought it would be beneficial for people to know the truth.

Work to gain wider and higher recognition as you are promoted

You can build great confidence and make bigger decisions as you face and overcome each problem, one by one. I am sure you know that you will be given heavier responsibilities as you are promoted. It is important, even for religious leaders, to work to gain wider and higher recognition.

For example, we recorded spiritual messages from Jesus Christ and the guardian spirit of the current pope, and there were differences in their way of thinking. So, the pope's guardian spirit was puzzled and wondered if he would no longer be a Christian if his opinion was different from Jesus's. He might be right. Considering his position, it would not be too good for him if Jesus's opinion was different from his. But many people want to know the truth, and we have the obligation to convey it to them.

Pope Francis is in the position to lead more than one billion Catholic believers, so he should listen to other people's opinions and correct his thinking where he should. Please note that we are trying to keep our tone down, so that we do not sound too disrespectful.

Leaders must take responsibility for their words and decisions

Happy Science is thinking from different points of view and working actively. In other words, some of the work that we do goes beyond the scope of religion, so it's very difficult work we are doing, but our priority is to build a better future for as many people as possible. We are a religious group with a distinguished organization, so people sometimes listen to us even when we say something that a single individual would be ignored for.

Current View on the Coronavirus Infection

The Happiness Realization Party presented a proposal to the government the other day, and our Party Leader released our ideas online. Due to this, the guardian spirit of Prime Minister Abe came to me last night, but he looked very anxious and wasn't Shinzo Abe, but "Shinro" Abe (a pun meaning "anxious" Abe). It's normal to be anxious. This is exactly how he would be because he doesn't know what to do.

It is natural for him to experience many happenings because he has held the position of prime minister for a long time. He has skillfully talked his way out of things, so he should just do his best this time, too. If he can't give his best

Jesus Christ's Answers to the Coronavirus Pandemic (Tokyo: HS Press, 2020)

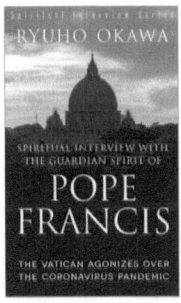

Spiritual Interview with the Guardian Spirit of Pope Francis: The Vatican Agonizes over the Coronavirus Pandemic (Tokyo: HS Press, 2020)

anymore, he will have no choice but to step down. Happy Science is not wanting to take all the responsibility (for the coronavirus-related issues). Be it Prime Minister Abe or Tokyo Governor Koike, including the other governors, I want them to take "responsibility for their speech" and "responsibility for their decisions" by themselves.

I cannot give them all the answers, but I will continue to provide materials that they can refer to.

Afterword

In this book, I'm not saying that you should disregard the prevention of coronavirus infection; do what you feel you have to do.

However, even if you stay at home for one or two months, the coronavirus pandemic will not disappear from this earth. It will spread to countries all over the world, with second and third waves to follow. You will need to survive by living with the coronavirus.

Basically, each of you must strengthen your immunity, produce wisdom, and restart your economic activities. If not, large businesses, nations, and municipalities will fail, and only hatred and sorrow will remain.

There is still no effective vaccine at this time, so please go back to the power of faith once again. Possession by a group of tiny viruses is basically no different from possession by evil spirits. If so, you can drive them away using the power of God or Buddha. With this book, you must fight against Grim Reapers.

Ryuho Okawa
Master & CEO of Happy Science Group
May 21, 2020

TRANSLATOR'S NOTES

1 Foxes and raccoon dogs are often depicted as being rivals in Japanese folklore.

2 Ultraman is a character who appears in the Japanese science fiction TV series. He has a finishing move called the "Specium Ray," which is fired from his hand when he crosses his arms.

3 One month after this book was published in Japan, the Japanese government abolished the meetings of experts they had set up to find ways to treat the novel coronavirus from a medical perspective. Instead, they began holding meetings where experts from various fields gathered.

4 Criteria in which the Japanese government proposed to prevent the spreading of the novel coronavirus. It tells people to avoid the following three: closed spaces with poor ventilation, crowded places with many people nearby, and close-contact settings such as close-range conversations.

Miracle Healing
—from Coronavirus Infection—

At Happy Science, many people around the world are curing not only from the coronavirus infection, but from cancer and other incurable diseases. We would like to introduce a testimony as well as *Kigan*—ritual prayers of Happy Science—which you can take to help yourself or your loved ones.

Testimony
MY UNCLE'S MIRACULOUS RECOVERY

On Aug. 10th, 2020, I heard that my uncle had been in a critical health condition for a week due to the infection of the coronavirus. He was unconscious and in the ICU where no visitors were allowed. As soon as I heard of his condition, I decided to take Kigan, **"Prayer for Defeating the Infection of Novel Coronavirus Originated in China"** *with my aunt, cousins, and my mother. The only thing we could do was to pray in such a situation and that was our only solution. Then, his condition improved greatly. By Aug. 15th he regained consciousness, and by the 18th, I was able to have a video chat with him. He looked completely normal and said, "This is definitely a miracle. I was unconscious but I surely felt the prayer. I realized how loved I was by many people, and how much I've already been given." The Kigan truly has the power to connect us to the Light. I thank you Lord.*

(Ms. D.E., Female, 20s)

Kigan for You

A vast variety of *Kigan* is available at Happy Science to suit your needs in life. Here are some *Kigan* that are related to the coronavirus problem.

Prayer for Defeating the Infection of Novel Coronavirus Originated in China

Prayer for Recovery from Illness

Prayer for Exorcising Evil Spirits

Prayer to Break Out of Economic Depression

How to Strengthen Your Immunity
Lecture DVD

This is the DVD of the lecture recorded in Chapter Two of this book. The spiritual power of this lecture DVD is more powerful than the book. So you are recommended to watch this many times to deepen your understanding.

➲ Available at **Happy Science local branches** and **shoja (temples) worldwide**. See p. 156.

ABOUT THE AUTHOR

RYUHO OKAWA was born on July 7th 1956, in Tokushima, Japan. After graduating from the University of Tokyo with a law degree, he joined a Tokyo-based trading house. While working at its New York headquarters, he studied international finance at the Graduate Center of the City University of New York. In 1981, he attained Great Enlightenment and became aware that he is El Cantare with a mission to bring salvation to all humankind. In 1986, he established Happy Science. It now has members in over 140 countries across the world, with more than 700 local branches and temples as well as 10,000 missionary houses around the world. The total number of lectures has exceeded 3,200 (of which more than 150 are in English) and over 2,750 books (of which more than 550 are Spiritual Interview Series) have been published, many of which are translated into 31 languages. Many of the books, including *The Laws of the Sun* have become best sellers or million sellers. To date, Happy Science has produced 21 movies. The original story and original concept were given by the Executive Producer Ryuho Okawa. Recent movie titles are *Living in the Age of Miracles* (documentary, Aug. 2020), *Twiceborn* (live-action, Oct. 2020), and *Utsukushiki-Yuwaku-Gendai-no-"Gahi"* (literally, "Beautiful Temptation: The Modern 'Painted Skin'," live-action movie scheduled to be released in 2021). He has also composed the lyrics and music of over 200 songs, such as theme songs and featured songs of movies. Moreover, he is the Founder of Happy Science University and Happy Science Academy (Junior and Senior High School), Founder and President of the Happiness Realization Party, Founder and Honorary Headmaster of Happy Science Institute of Government and Management, Founder of IRH Press Co., Ltd., and the Chairperson of New Star Production Co., Ltd. and ARI Production Co., Ltd.

WHAT IS EL CANTARE?

El Cantare means "the Light of the Earth," and is the Supreme God of the Earth who has been guiding humankind since the beginning of Genesis. He is whom Jesus called Father and Muhammad called Allah. Different parts of El Cantare's core consciousness have descended to Earth in the past, once as Alpha and another as Elohim. His branch spirits, such as Shakyamuni Buddha and Hermes, have descended to Earth many times and helped to flourish many civilizations. To unite various religions and to integrate various fields of study in order to build a new civilization on Earth, a part of the core consciousness has descended to Earth as Master Ryuho Okawa.

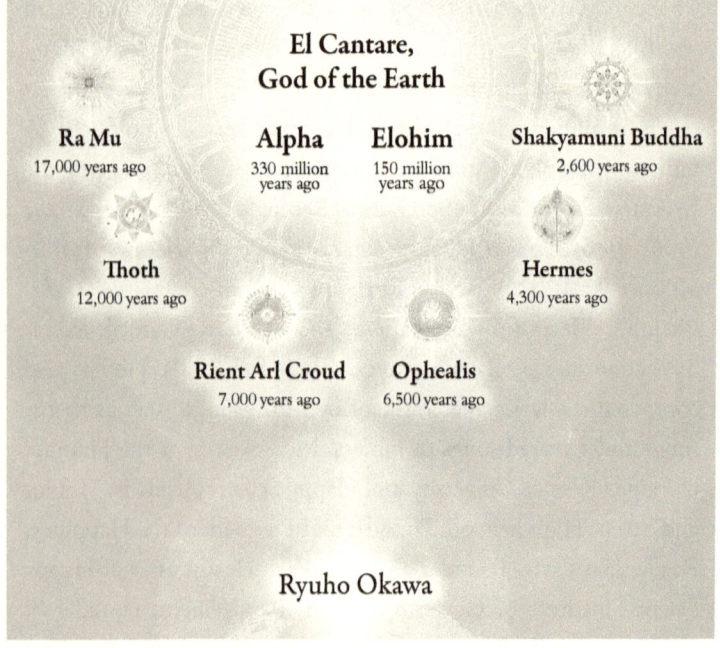

Alpha is a part of the core consciousness of El Cantare who descended to Earth around 330 million years ago. Alpha preached Earth's Truths to harmonize and unify Earth-born humans and space people who came from other planets.

Elohim is a part of El Cantare's core consciousness who descended to Earth around 150 million years ago. He gave wisdom, mainly on the differences of light and darkness, good and evil.

Shakyamuni Buddha was born as a prince into the Shakya Clan in India around 2,600 years ago. When he was 29 years old, he renounced the world and sought enlightenment. He later attained Great Enlightenment and founded Buddhism.

Hermes is one of the 12 Olympian gods in Greek mythology, but the spiritual Truth is that he taught the teachings of love and progress around 4,300 years ago that became the origin of the current Western civilization. He is a hero that truly existed.

Ophealis was born in Greece around 6,500 years ago and was the leader who took an expedition to as far as Egypt. He is the God of miracles, prosperity, and arts, and is known as Osiris in the Egyptian mythology.

Rient Arl Croud was born as a king of the ancient Incan Empire around 7,000 years ago and taught about the mysteries of the mind. In the heavenly world, he is responsible for the interactions that take place between various planets.

Thoth was an almighty leader who built the golden age of the Atlantic civilization around 12,000 years ago. In the Egyptian mythology, he is known as god Thoth.

Ra Mu was a leader who built the golden age of the civilization of Mu around 17,000 years ago. As a religious leader and a politician, he ruled by uniting religion and politics.

WHAT IS A SPIRITUAL MESSAGE?

We are all spiritual beings living on this earth. The following is the mechanism behind Master Ryuho Okawa's spiritual messages.

1 You are a spirit

People are born into this world to gain wisdom through various experiences and return to the other world when their lives end. We are all spirits and repeat this cycle in order to refine our souls.

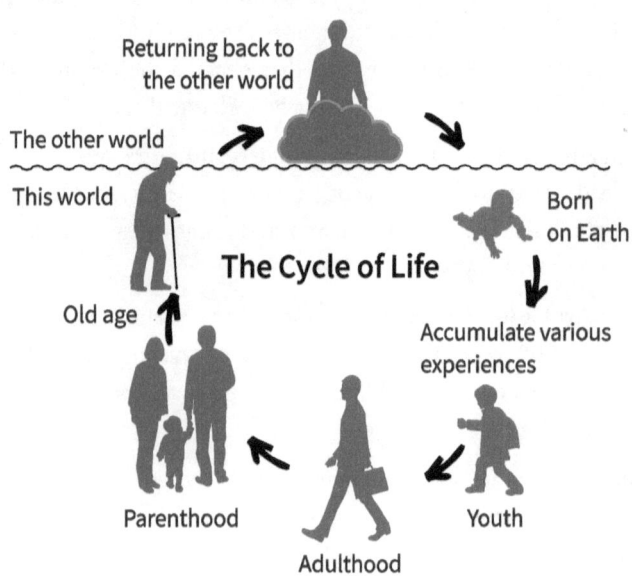

2 You have a guardian spirit

Guardian spirits are those who protect the people who are living on this earth. Each of us has a guardian spirit that watches over us and guides us from the other world. They were us in our past life, and are identical in how we think.

3 How spiritual messages work

Master Ryuho Okawa, through his enlightenment, is capable of summoning any spirit from anywhere in the world, including the spirit world.

Master Okawa's way of receiving spiritual messages is fundamentally different from that of other psychic mediums who undergo trances and are thereby completely taken over by the spirits they are channeling.

Master Okawa's attainment of a high level of enlightenment enables him to retain full control of his consciousness and body throughout the duration of the spiritual message. To allow the spirits to express their own thoughts and personalities freely, however, Master Okawa usually softens the dominancy of his consciousness. This way, he is able to keep his own philosophies out of the way and ensure that the spiritual messages are pure expressions of the spirits he is channeling.

Since guardian spirits think at the same subconscious level as the person living on earth, Master Okawa can summon the spirit and find out what the person on earth is actually thinking. If the person has already returned to the other world, the spirit can give messages to the people living on earth through Master Okawa.

Since 2009, more than 1,100 sessions of spiritual messages have been openly recorded by Master Okawa, and the majority of these have been published. Spiritual messages from the guardian spirits of people living today such as Donald Trump, Joe Biden, Boris Johnson, Angela Merkel, Vladimir Putin, and Xi Jinping, as well as spiritual messages sent from the spirit world by Jesus Christ, Muhammad, Thomas Edison, Mother Teresa, Steve Jobs and Nelson Mandela are just a tiny pack of spiritual messages that were published so far.

Domestically, in Japan, these spiritual messages are being read by a wide range of politicians and mass media, and the high-level contents of these books are delivering an impact even more on politics, news and public opinion. In recent years, there have been spiritual messages recorded in English, and English translations are being done on the spiritual messages given in Japanese. These have been published overseas, one after another, and have started to shake the world.

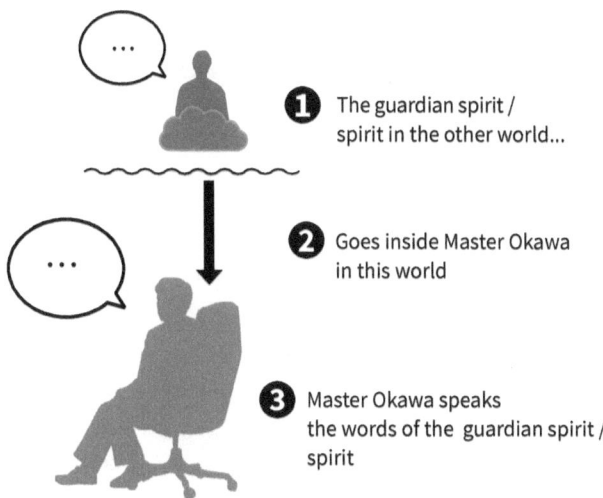

*For more about spiritual messages and a complete list of books in the Spiritual Interview Series, visit **okawabooks.com***

ABOUT HAPPY SCIENCE

Happy Science is a global movement that empowers individuals to find purpose and spiritual happiness and to share that happiness with their families, societies, and the world. With more than 12 million members around the world, Happy Science aims to increase awareness of spiritual truths and expand our capacity for love, compassion, and joy so that together we can create the kind of world we all wish to live in.

Activities at Happy Science are based on the Principles of Happiness (Love, Wisdom, Self-Reflection, and Progress). These principles embrace worldwide philosophies and beliefs, transcending boundaries of culture and religions.

> **Love** teaches us to give ourselves freely without expecting anything in return; it encompasses giving, nurturing, and forgiving.

> **Wisdom** leads us to the insights of spiritual truths, and opens us to the true meaning of life and the will of God (the universe, the highest power, Buddha).

> **Self-Reflection** brings a mindful, nonjudgmental lens to our thoughts and actions to help us find our truest selves—the essence of our souls—and deepen our connection to the highest power. It helps us attain a clean and peaceful mind and leads us to the right life path.

Progress emphasizes the positive, dynamic aspects of our spiritual growth—actions we can take to manifest and spread happiness around the world. It's a path that not only expands our soul growth, but also furthers the collective potential of the world we live in.

PROGRAMS AND EVENTS

The doors of Happy Science are open to all. We offer a variety of programs and events, including self-exploration and self-growth programs, spiritual seminars, meditation and contemplation sessions, study groups, and book events.

Our programs are designed to:
* Deepen your understanding of your purpose and meaning in life
* Improve your relationships and increase your capacity to love unconditionally
* Attain peace of mind, decrease anxiety and stress, and feel positive
* Gain deeper insights and a broader perspective on the world
* Learn how to overcome life's challenges

... and much more.

*For more information, visit **happy-science.org**.*

OUR ACTIVITIES

Happy Science does other various activities to provide support for those in need.

◆ **You Are An Angel! General Incorporated Association**
Happy Science has a volunteer network in Japan that encourages and supports children with disabilities as well as their parents and guardians.

◆ **Never Mind School for Truancy**
At 'Never Mind,' we support students who find it very challenging to attend schools in Japan. We also nurture their self-help spirit and power to rebound against obstacles in life based on Master Okawa's teachings and faith.

◆ **"Prevention Against Suicide" Campaign since 2003**
A nationwide campaign to reduce suicides; over 20,000 people commit suicide every year in Japan. "The Suicide Prevention Website-Words of Truth for You-" presents spiritual prescriptions for worries such as depression, lost love, extramarital affairs, bullying and work-related problems, thereby saving many lives.

◆ **Support for Anti-bullying Campaigns**
Happy Science provides support for a group of parents and guardians, Network to Protect Children from Bullying, a general incorporated foundation launched in Japan to end bullying, including those that can even be called a criminal offense. So far, the network received more than 5,000 cases and resolved 90% of them.

- **The Golden Age Scholarship**
  This scholarship is granted to students who can contribute greatly and bring a hopeful future to the world.

- **Success No.1**
  Buddha's Truth Afterschool Academy
  Happy Science has over 180 classrooms throughout Japan and in several cities around the world that focus on afterschool education for children. The education focuses on faith and morals in addition to supporting children's school studies.

- **Angel Plan V**
  For children under the age of kindergarten, Happy Science holds classes for nurturing healthy, positive, and creative boys and girls.

- **Future Stars Training Department**
  The Future Stars Training Department was founded within the Happy Science Media Division with the goal of nurturing talented individuals to become successful in the performing arts and entertainment industry.

- **New Star Production Co., Ltd.**
  ARI Production Co., Ltd.
  We have companies to nurture actors and actresses, artists, and vocalists. They are also involved in film production.

ABOUT HAPPY SCIENCE MOVIES

TWICEBORN

STORY Satoru Ichijo receives a message from the spiritual world and realizes his mission is to lead humankind to happiness. He became a successful businessman while publishing spiritual messages secretly, but the devil's temptation shakes his mind and...

33 Awards from 7 Countries!

...and more!

*For more information, visit **www.twicebornmovie.com***

LIVING IN THE AGE OF MIRACLES

An inspirational documentary about two Japanese actors meeting people who experienced miracles in their lives. Through their quest, they find the key to working miracles and learn what "living in the age of miracles" truly means.

7 Awards from 2 Countries!

...and more!

IMMORTAL HERO On VOD NOW

Based on the true story of a man whose near-death experience inspires him to choose life... and change the lives of millions.

41 Awards from 9 Countries!

SPAIN
BARCELONA INTERNATIONAL FILM FESTIVAL 2019
[THE CASTELL AWARDS]

SPAIN
MADRID INTERNATIONAL FILM FESTIVAL 2019
[BEST DIRECTOR OF A FOREIGN LANGUAGE FEATURE FILM]

ITALY
FLORENCE FILM AWARDS JUL 2019
[HONORABLE MENTION: FEATURE FILM]

USA
INDIE VISIONS FILM FESTIVAL JUL 2019 [WINNER (NARRATIVE FEATURE FILM)]

ITALY
FLORENCE FILM AWARDS JUL 2019
[BEST ORIGINAL SCREENPLAY]

ITALY
DIAMOND FILM AWARDS JUL 2019 [WINNER (NARRATIVE FEATURE FILM)]

...and more!

For more information, visit ***www.immortal-hero.com***

THE REAL EXORCIST On VOD NOW

56 Awards from 9 Countries!

STORY Tokyo —the most mystical city in the world where you find spiritual spots in the most unexpected places. Sayuri works as a part-time waitress at a small coffee shop "Extra" where regular customers enjoy the authentic coffee that the owner brews. Meanwhile, Sayuri uses her supernatural powers to help those who are troubled by spiritual phenomena one after another. Through her special consultations, she touches the hearts of the people and helps them by showing the truths of the invisible world.

USA
GOLD REMI AWARD
53rd WorldFest Houston International Film Festival 2020

MONACO
BEST FEATURE FILM
17th Angel Film Awards 2020
Monaco International Film Festival

BEST FEMALE ACTOR
17th Angel Film Awards 2020
Monaco International Film Festival

NIGERIA
BEST FEATURE FILM
EKO International Film Festival 2020

BEST FEMALE SUPPORTING ACTOR
17th Angel Film Awards 2020
Monaco International Film Festival

BEST SUPPORTING ACTRESS
EKO International Film Festival 2020

BEST VISUAL EFFECTS
17th Angel Film Awards 2020
Monaco International Film Festival

...and more!

For more information, visit ***www.realexorcistmovie.com***

CONTACT INFORMATION

Happy Science is a worldwide organization with faith centers around the globe. For a comprehensive list of centers, visit the worldwide directory at ***happy-science.org***. The following are some of the many Happy Science locations:

UNITED STATES AND CANADA

New York
79 Franklin St., New York, NY 10013
Phone: 212-343-7972
Fax: 212-343-7973
Email: ny@happy-science.org
Website: happyscience-na.org

New Jersey
725 River Rd, #102B, Edgewater, NJ 07020
Phone: 201-313-0127
Fax: 201-313-0120
Email: nj@happy-science.org
Website: happyscience-na.org

Florida
5208 8th St., St. Zephyrhills, FL 33542
Phone: 813-715-0000
Fax: 813-715-0010
Email: florida@happy-science.org
Website: happyscience-na.org

Atlanta
1874 Piedmont Ave., NE Suite 360-C
Atlanta, GA 30324
Phone: 404-892-7770
Email: atlanta@happy-science.org
Website: happyscience-na.org

San Francisco
525 Clinton St.
Redwood City, CA 94062
Phone & Fax: 650-363-2777
Email: sf@happy-science.org
Website: happyscience-na.org

Los Angeles
1590 E. Del Mar Blvd., Pasadena, CA 91106
Phone: 626-395-7775
Fax: 626-395-7776
Email: la@happy-science.org
Website: happyscience-na.org

Orange County
10231 Slater Ave., #204
Fountain Valley, CA 92708
Phone: 714-745-1140
Email: oc@happy-science.org
Website: happyscience-na.org

San Diego
7841 Balboa Ave., Suite #202
San Diego, CA 92111
Phone: 626-395-7775
Fax: 626-395-7776
E-mail: sandiego@happy-science.org
Website: happyscience-na.org

Hawaii
Phone: 808-591-9772
Fax: 808-591-9776
Email: hi@happy-science.org
Website: happyscience-na.org

Kauai
3343 Kanakolu Street, Suite 5
Lihue, HI 96766, U.S.A.
Phone: 808-822-7007
Fax: 808-822-6007
Email: kauai-hi@happy-science.org
Website: kauai.happyscience-na.org

Toronto
845 The Queensway
Etobicoke ON M8Z 1N6 Canada
Phone: 1-416-901-3747
Email: toronto@happy-science.org
Website: happy-science.ca

Vancouver
#201-2607 East 49th Avenue
Vancouver, BC, V5S 1J9, Canada
Phone: 1-604-437-7735
Fax: 1-604-437-7764
Email: vancouver@happy-science.org
Website: happy-science.ca

INTERNATIONAL

Tokyo
1-6-7 Togoshi, Shinagawa
Tokyo, 142-0041 Japan
Phone: 81-3-6384-5770
Fax: 81-3-6384-5776
Email: tokyo@happy-science.org
Website: happy-science.org

Seoul
74, Sadang-ro 27-gil,
Dongjak-gu, Seoul, Korea
Phone: 82-2-3478-8777
Fax: 82-2-3478-9777
Email: korea@happy-science.org
Website: happyscience-korea.org

London
3 Margaret St.
London,W1W 8RE United Kingdom
Phone: 44-20-7323-9255
Fax: 44-20-7323-9344
Email: eu@happy-science.org
Website: happyscience-uk.org

Taipei
No. 89, Lane 155, Dunhua N. Road
Songshan District, Taipei City 105, Taiwan
Phone: 886-2-2719-9377
Fax: 886-2-2719-5570
Email: taiwan@happy-science.org
Website: happyscience-tw.org

Sydney
516 Pacific Hwy, Lane Cove North,
NSW 2066, Australia
Phone: 61-2-9411-2877
Fax: 61-2-9411-2822
Email: sydney@happy-science.org

Malaysia
No 22A, Block 2, Jalil Link Jalan Jalil Jaya 2,
Bukit Jalil 57000, Kuala Lumpur, Malaysia
Phone: 60-3-8998-7877
Fax: 60-3-8998-7977
Email: malaysia@happy-science.org
Website: happyscience.org.my

Brazil Headquarters
Rua. Domingos de Morais 1154,
Vila Mariana, Sao Paulo SP
CEP 04009-002, Brazil
Phone: 55-11-5088-3800
Fax: 55-11-5088-3806
Email: sp@happy-science.org
Website: happyscience.com.br

Nepal
Kathmandu Metropolitan City Ward
No. 15,
Ring Road, Kimdol,
Sitapaila Kathmandu, Nepal
Phone: 97-714-272931
Email: nepal@happy-science.org

Jundiai
Rua Congo, 447, Jd. Bonfiglioli
Jundiai-CEP, 13207-340
Phone: 55-11-4587-5952
Email: jundiai@happy-science.org

Uganda
Plot 877 Rubaga Road, Kampala
P.O. Box 34130, Kampala, Uganda
Phone: 256-79-4682-121
Email: uganda@happy-science.org
Website: happyscience-uganda.org

ABOUT HAPPINESS REALIZATION PARTY

The Happiness Realization Party (HRP) was founded in May 2009 by Master Ryuho Okawa as part of the Happy Science Group to offer concrete and proactive solutions to the current issues such as military threats from North Korea and China and the long-term economic recession. HRP aims to implement drastic reforms of the Japanese government, thereby bringing peace and prosperity to Japan. To accomplish this, HRP proposes two key policies:

1) Strengthening the national security and the Japan-U.S. alliance, which plays a vital role in the stability of Asia.

2) Improving the Japanese economy by implementing drastic tax cuts, taking monetary easing measures and creating new major industries.

HRP advocates that Japan should offer a model of a religious nation that allows diverse values and beliefs to coexist, and that contributes to global peace.

*For more information, visit **en.hr-party.jp***

ABOUT IRH PRESS USA

IRH Press USA Inc. was founded in 2013 as an affiliated firm of IRH Press Co., Ltd. Based in New York, the press publishes books in various categories including spirituality, religion, and self-improvement and publishes books by Ryuho Okawa, the author of over 100 million books sold worldwide. For more information, visit *okawabooks.com*.

Follow us on:
Facebook: Okawa Books   **Twitter:** Okawa Books
Goodreads: Ryuho Okawa   **Instagram:** OkawaBooks
Pinterest: Okawa Books

---- **MEDIA** ----

OKAWA BOOK CLUB

A conversation about Ryuho Okawa's titles, topics ranging from self-help, current affairs, spirituality and religions.

Available at iTunes, Spotify and Amazon Music.

Apple iTunes:
https://podcasts.apple.com/us/podcast/okawa-book-club/id1527893043

Spotify:
https://open.spotify.com/show/09mpgX2iJ6stVm4eBRdo2b

Amazon Music:
https://music.amazon.com/podcasts/7b759f24-ff72-4523-bfee-24f48294998f/Okawa-Book-Club

BOOKS BY RYUHO OKAWA

RYUHO OKAWA'S LAWS SERIES

The Laws Series is an annual volume of books that are mainly comprised of Ryuho Okawa's lectures on various topics that highlight principles and guidelines for the activities of Happy Science every year. *The Laws of the Sun*, the first publication of the laws series in 1987, ranked in the annual best-selling list in Japan. Since then, all of the laws series' titles have ranked in the annual best-selling list for more than two decades, setting socio-cultural trends in Japan and around the world.

The 26th Laws Series

THE LAWS OF STEEL

LIVING A LIFE OF RESILIENCE, CONFIDENCE AND PROSPERITY

Paperback • 256 pages • $16.95
ISBN: 978-1-942125-65-5

This book is a compilation of six lectures that Ryuho Okawa gave in 2018 and 2019, each containing passionate messages for us to open a brighter future. This powerful and inspiring book will not only show us the ways to achieve true happiness and prosperity, but also the ways to solve many global issues we now face. It presents us with wisdom that is based on a spiritual perspective, and a new design for our future society. Through this book, we can overcome differences in values and create a peaceful world, thereby ushering in a Golden Age.

For a complete list of books, visit **okawabooks.com**

THE TRILOGY

The first three volumes of the Laws Series, *The Laws of the Sun*, *The Golden Laws*, and *The Nine Dimensions* make a trilogy that completes the basic framework of the teachings of God's Truths. *The Laws of the Sun* discusses the structure of God's Laws, *The Golden Laws* expounds on the doctrine of time, and *The Nine Dimensions* reveals the nature of space.

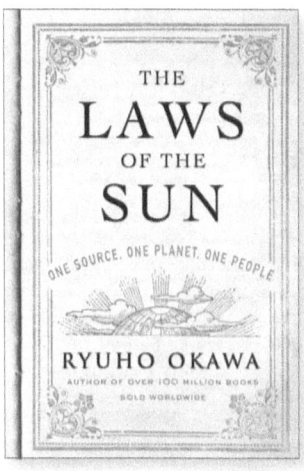

THE LAWS OF THE SUN
ONE SOURCE, ONE PLANET, ONE PEOPLE

Paperback • 288 pages • $15.95
ISBN: 978-1-942125-43-3

IMAGINE IF YOU COULD ASK GOD why He created this world and what spiritual laws He used to shape us—and everything around us. If we could understand His designs and intentions, we could discover what our goals in life should be and whether our actions move us closer to those goals or farther away.

At a young age, a spiritual calling prompted Ryuho Okawa to outline what he innately understood to be universal truths for all humankind. In *The Laws of the Sun*, Okawa outlines these laws of the universe and provides a road map for living one's life with greater purpose and meaning.

In this powerful book, Ryuho Okawa reveals the transcendent nature of consciousness and the secrets of our multidimensional universe and our place in it. By understanding the different stages of love and following the Buddhist Eightfold Path, he believes we can speed up our eternal process of development. *The Laws of the Sun* shows the way to realize true happiness—a happiness that continues from this world through the other.

---

*For a complete list of books, visit **okawabooks.com***

THE GOLDEN LAWS
HISTORY THROUGH THE EYES OF THE ETERNAL BUDDHA

Paperback • 201 pages • $14.95
ISBN: 978-1-941779-81-1

Throughout history, Great Guiding Spirits of Light have been present on Earth in both the East and the West at crucial points in human history to further our spiritual development. *The Golden Laws* reveals how Divine Plan has been unfolding on Earth, and outlines 5,000 years of the secret history of humankind.

THE NINE DIMENSIONS
UNVEILING THE LAWS OF ETERNITY

Paperback • 168 pages • $15.95
ISBN: 978-0-982698-56-3

This book is a window into the mind of our loving God. When the religions and cultures of the world discover the truth of their common spiritual origin, they will be inspired to accept their differences, come together under faith in God, and build an era of harmony and peaceful progress on Earth.

THE LAWS OF HAPPINESS
LOVE, WISDOM, SELF-REFLECTION AND PROGRESS

Paperback • 264 pages • $16.95
ISBN: 978-1-942125-70-9

What is happiness? In this book, Ryuho Okawa explains that happiness is not found outside us; it's found within us, in how we think, how we look at our lives in this world, what we believe in, and how we devote our hearts to the work we do. Even as we go through suffering and unfavorable circumstances, we can always shift our mindset and become happier by simply *giving love* instead of *taking love*.

---

*For a complete list of books, visit **okawabooks.com***

THE LAWS OF SUCCESS
A SPIRITUAL GUIDE TO TURNING YOUR HOPES INTO REALITY

Paperback • 208 pages • $15.95
ISBN: 978-1-942125-15-0

The Laws of Success offers 8 spiritual principles that, when put to practice in our day-to-day life, will help us attain lasting success. The timeless wisdom and practical steps that Ryuho Okawa offers will guide us through any difficulties and problems we may face in life, and serve as guiding principles for living a positive, constructive, and meaningful life.

THE LAWS OF INVINCIBLE LEADERSHIP
AN EMPOWERING GUIDE FOR CONTINUOUS AND LASTING SUCCESS IN BUSINESS AND IN LIFE

Hardcover • 224 pages • $19.95
ISBN: 978-1-942125-30-3

Ryuho Okawa shares essential principles for all who wish to become invincible managers and leaders in their fields of work, organizations, societies, and nations. Your keys to becoming an invincible overall winner in life and in business are just pages away.

THE LAWS OF FAITH
ONE WORLD BEYOND DIFFERENCES

Paperback • 208 pages • $15.95
ISBN: 978-1-942125-34-1

Ryuho Okawa preaches at the core of a new universal religion from various angles while integrating logical and spiritual viewpoints in mind with current world situations. This book offers us the key to accept diversities beyond differences to create a world filled with peace and prosperity.

---

*For a complete list of books, visit **okawabooks.com***

THE NOVEL CORONAVIRUS INFECTION, THE FUTURE PREDICTION TO HUMANKIND

WITH SAVIOR
MESSAGES FROM SPACE BEING YAIDRON

Paperback • 232 pages • $13.95
ISBN: 978-1-943869-94-7

The human race is now faced with multiple unprecedented crises. Perhaps God is warning us humans to reconsider our materialistic and arrogant ways. Fortunately, God has sent us a savior, who is now teaching us to repent and showing us the path we should choose. In this book, space being Yaidron sends his warnings and messages of hope.

JESUS CHRIST'S ANSWERS TO THE CORONAVIRUS PANDEMIC

Paperback • 204 pages • $11.95
ISBN: 978-1-943869-81-7

In this book, the spirit of Jesus answers the causes, prospects, and coping strategies for the novel coronavirus pandemic. Instead of hoping for the development of an effective vaccine to come soon, we should use our spiritual power to defeat the evil thoughts that spiritually possess this virus. It's a book for all who believe in Jesus.

SHAKYAMUNI BUDDHA'S FUTURE PREDICTION

Paperback • 213 pages • $13.95
ISBN: 978-1-943869-91-6

In this book, the spirits of Shakyamuni Buddha and John Lennon warn us about the troubles that await humankind, require us who live today to reflect on the arrogance of belittling God, and teach us how to overcome difficulties. What the world needs now are many people who work as a part of God's power. You, too, can become a part of the power to save the world.

---

*For a complete list of books, visit **okawabooks.com***

What Will Become of Coronavirus Pandemic?

Readings by Edgar Cayce

Paperback • 86 pages • $9.95
ISBN: 978-1-943869-82-4

Edgar Cayce, now a spirit in heaven, tells us that the novel coronavirus infection is likely to spread even further, but he also teaches us the truth behind it and how to deal with it. But you, yourself, can gain the power to defeat the novel coronavirus. Here is your light of hope.

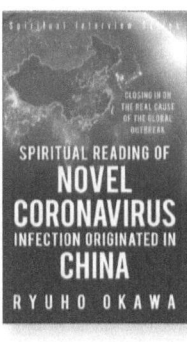

Spiritual Reading of Novel Coronavirus Infection Originated in China

Closing in on the real cause of the global outbreak

Paperback • 278 pages • $13.95
ISBN: 978-1-943869-77-0

This worldwide pandemic is not a mere act of nature nor a coincidence, but rather, heaven's warning to humanity, especially China. Through this book, you can find out "the immunity" against the novel coronavirus, among other shocking truths.

The Novel Coronavirus Originated in China: Lessons for Humankind

Spiritual messages from Shibasaburo Kitasato and R. A. Goal

Paperback • 228 pages • $13.95
ISBN: 978-1-943869-88-6

This book records spiritual messages from a bacteriologist and a space being. They disclose many truths about the novel coronavirus pandemic, such as China's hidden secrets, what the future holds, and hopeful messages for humanity. Only when humanity learns what we are to learn from this pandemic, can we escape this worldwide crisis and create a new age.

---

*For a complete list of books, visit **okawabooks.com***

TO SURVIVE IN THE AGE OF CRISIS

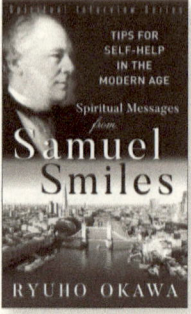

SPIRITUAL MESSAGES FROM SAMUEL SMILES
TIPS FOR SELF-HELP IN THE MODERN AGE

Paperback • 182 pages • $11.95
ISBN: 978-1-943869-69-5

If Smiles was alive today and saw what the world has come to, what would he think and say? What kind of advice would he give to his home country, Britain, seeing the state it is in over the Brexit issue? The answers to these questions are in this very book.

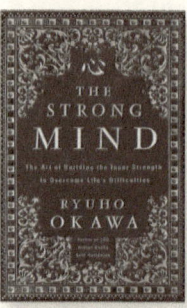

THE STRONG MIND
THE ART OF BUILDING THE INNER STRENGTH TO OVERCOME LIFE'S DIFFICULTIES

Paperback • 192 pages • $15.95
ISBN: 978-1-942125-36-5

The strong mind is what we need to rise time and again, and to move forward no matter what difficulties we face in life. This book will inspire and empower you to take courage, develop a mature and cultivated heart, and achieve resilience and hardiness so that you can break through the barriers of your limits and keep winning in the battle of your life.

INVINCIBLE THINKING
AN ESSENTIAL GUIDE FOR A LIFETIME OF GROWTH, SUCCESS, AND TRIUMPH

Hardcover • 208 pages • $16.95
ISBN: 978-1-942125-25-9

In this book, Ryuho Okawa lays out the principles of invincible thinking that will allow us to achieve long-lasting triumph. This powerful and unique philosophy is not only about becoming successful or achieving our goal in life, but also about building the foundation of life that becomes the basis of our life-long, lasting success and happiness.

For a complete list of books, visit **okawabooks.com**

www.ingramcontent.com/pod-product-compliance
Lightning Source LLC
Chambersburg PA
CBHW030152100526
44592CB00009B/236